Jan Bowen is renowned for her ability to express the law in a way clearly understood by the non-lawyer. Her 25 books include the best-selling *The Macquarie Easy Guide to Australian Law*, *The Reader's Digest Legal Question and Answer Book* and *Your Business and the Law*. She has been at the forefront of the movement towards plain English and the law, first with the Law Foundation of New South Wales and then with the Law Society of New South Wales. She now runs her own consultancy, Plain English Communications, which advises all manner of businesses, both large and small, on how to communicate in a way that people can understand. To keep life interesting, Jan has also been a columnist with the *Australian Women's Weekly*, writes travel books, and has authored three interview/profile books, *The Fabulous Fifties*, *Men Talk* and *Feminists Fatale*. Jan Bowen lives in Sydney with her husband and has three sons.

Love and the LAW

Jan Bowen

ALLEN & UNWIN

First published in 2000 by
Allen & Unwin
9 Atchison Street
St Leonards NSW 1590
Australia
Phone: (61 2) 8425 0100
Fax: (61 2) 9906 2218
E-mail: frontdesk@allen-unwin.com.au
Web: http://www.allen-unwin.com.au

National Library of Australia
Cataloguing-in-Publication entry:

Bowen, Jan.
Love and the law.

Includes index.
ISBN 1 86508 170 1.

1. Family law—Australia. 2. Family—Australia.
3. Marriage—Australia.

346.94015

Set in 11.5/14 pt Adobe Caslon by Bookhouse Digital, Sydney
Printed by SRM Production Services Sdn Bhd, Malaysia

10 9 8 7 6 5 4 3 2 1

CONTENTS

Introduction vii

Part one: Getting together

1 Love and living together 3
2 Love and marriage 16
3 Same-sex relationships 30

Part two: Having children

4 Having a baby 43
5 Bringing up children 57

Part three: When love flies out the window

6 Ending a marriage 71
7 Ending a de facto relationship 96
8 When parents separate 103

Part four: Fundamentals

9 Money 119
10 Sex 138
11 Violence 148

Part five: Ageing and death

12 Growing older 159
13 Love and death 177

Part six: The legal system

14 The courts 195
15 Getting legal advice 203

Index 208

INTRODUCTION

Not many of us think of love as having much connection with the law. Quite the contrary in fact. In western cultures, at least, most of us subscribe to the ideal of romantic love in which we are swept off our feet by the object of our affections and carried along on a tide of emotion, letting the practical aspects of building a relationship take care of themselves.

The fact is that all but the most casual of romantic relationships are defined by a legal framework. At its most fundamental level, marriage is a contract which bestows rights and obligations regarding support. Increasingly, de facto relationships involve similar rights and obligations. If a marriage or de facto relationship ends, certain legal consequences flow from that. If children are involved parents must maintain them or the law may intervene.

The notion that love and the law are mutually exclusive is probably most evident in relation to money. The rising divorce rate may have made people a little more cautious but there is still a feeling that giving any more than a cursory consideration to financial arrangements before embarking on a relationship or marriage displays a mercenary nature and a lack of trust. While I was writing this book, I read a letter to a financial columnist in one of the major metropolitan newspapers from a woman asking for advice on what kind of financial agreement she and her fiancé should enter into as she wished to avoid the unpleasant disputes over money matters that had arisen when her first marriage ended. The reply was a terse reprimand from the adviser that such an avaricious approach boded ill for the marriage, it implied that she didn't really love her prospective husband and perhaps she should reconsider. This, in the late 1990s!

Looking back a mere twenty-five years, it is impossible not to be struck not only by the social expectations which restricted women but by the number of laws that dictated what women could and could not do, especially when they embarked on the relationship of marriage.

When a woman married she was generally expected to give up work. If a woman worked in the public service, once she married she was required by law to leave. If a woman became pregnant she was expected to resign or there was a high probability that she would be sacked—and she had no avenue of redress.

In the area of family planning, the pill was only just becoming accepted, other forms of contraception were unreliable and abortion was illegal—so backyard abortionists flourished and many women died or suffered permanent injury as a result of either incompetence or lack of proper hygiene.

The divorce law was based on fault and whoever left a marriage was the party at fault, no matter how justified their action may have been. Although the resultant social opprobrium was directed at both women and men, it was women who most frequently found themselves in dire financial straits. Unheard of was the concept that the family assets should be divided equitably and that a woman contributed to those assets by looking after the home and children. The man earned the money, so the money was his. The notion that decisions should be made with the 'best interests of the child' as the paramount consideration had not been thought of—so if a woman left she risked losing her children as 'punishment' for her iniquitous behaviour. The suffering that this might cause the children was not a consideration.

Because few women remained in the workforce once they married, they quickly lost whatever job skills they may once have had. This, combined with the fact that women weren't generally accepted in the workplace, meant that getting a job, and certainly a job that paid enough to live on, was difficult. Women could be refused a job or entry to a training course simply because they were women.

If a woman lived with a man without being married, she had virtually no rights. If the relationship broke down, she was often left destitute with no legal redress. If her children were born 'out of wedlock', as the saying went, the children were stigmatised, they had few rights of support from the father and no right to claim under the inheritance laws.

The social changes that have taken place in the last quarter of the twentieth century have been astonishing. Arguably we have lived through the greatest social revolution in human history. Perhaps only the industrial revolution can compete with it for impact. In response to these changes, the law has also been forced to evolve. Today, women's contribution to marriage is clearly acknowledged, even the contribution of a woman who stays at home to look after the family, in the laws relating to division of property on divorce. By and large, abortion is readily available without fear of adverse legal ramifications. Women's taken-for-granted participation in the workforce, whether they are married or single, is underpinned by antidiscrimination laws. No longer can a woman be denied a job simply because she is a woman or because she is married. Nor can she be denied a job if she isn't married but simply lives with her partner.

Children too have benefited from changing social attitudes.

There is now no legal distinction between a child born within a marriage and a child born to a couple who are not married. Decisions about children, if their parents' relationship breaks down, are based on the children's best interests and not on the behaviour of their parents.

This is a book for both men and women, but the simple fact is that, especially in the context of their relationships with men, it is women who have gained most from developments in the law since the previous turn of the century. Nevertheless, despite all the advances that have been made, the law is a turtle not a hare and the pace is sometimes frustratingly slow. Furthermore, the law is administered by human beings with all the human failings that implies. In the course of researching this book, I read of a Scottish judge who said, when he admonished a husband for striking his wife on the jaw, 'it is a well-known fact that you can strike your wife's bottom if you wish, but you must not strike her on the face', adding kindly, 'I believe that reasonable chastisement should be the duty of every husband if his wife misbehaves'. Did he say this a hundred years ago? No, it was little more than twenty years ago, in 1978, when women who are now only in their forties were just getting married.

Even more recently, in a celebrated judgment in South Australia, a judge noted that if a wife refused to engage in sex, her husband was entitled to 'use a measure of rougher than usual handling' to 'persuade' her. Or again, a Victorian judge hearing a case of sexual assault maintained that it was a well-known fact that 'when women said "no" they did not always mean "no"'.

Thankfully, as we approach the new millennium, such incidents are becoming less common. It is to be hoped that before the next century is too far advanced they will be seen as historical anachronisms.

Whether we realise it or not, the law touches on just about every aspect of love. We need a licence to get married, we must register a child's birth, certain rights and obligations are implied if we start living together, If we marry, those rights and obligations are even more extensive and legal responsibilities are imposed on us as parents. The law impinges on our relationship with our spouse, with our children, with our parents, with our de facto partner, with our same-sex partner.

It is vital to be aware of how the law affects our relationships so that we can control our life and protect ourselves from later problems, no matter how unlikely they may seem in the early flush of a new romance. The more we know about how the law works, the more we can save time and money and alleviate the possibility of emotional pain.

This book tries to give a general picture of the law as it relates to us in our loving relationships. There are chapters on marriage, divorce, de facto relationships, same-sex relationships, and our relationships as we get older ourselves or have to deal with ageing parents; other chapters relate to having a baby, our relationship with our children, the impact of the law on sex, and the legal implications of our financial arrangements. Of course, whole shelves of books have been written about each of these subjects and even practising lawyers aren't experts on every aspect of the law. Furthermore, because of our federal system, many laws vary according to the state in which we live. Some states are more progressive than others, some states use different terminology and some states have different practices and procedures. A precise statement of the law covering every jurisdiction and situation would defeat the purpose of providing an accessible, readable, ready reference.

Consequently, *Love and the Law* doesn't mean you won't need legal advice. Indeed, if you have a legal problem, you are urged to get prompt legal advice about that particular problem, since no written text can possibly take account of the individual circumstances that apply in your case. What it is hoped *Love and the Law* will do is help you conduct your human relationships in a way that will avoid legal problems arising, give you a basis for asserting your rights if you need to, recognise when the time has come to consult a lawyer and, when you do consult a lawyer, enable you to save time and money by being a more informed consumer.

Jan Bowen

part one

Getting together

chapter one

LOVE AND LIVING TOGETHER

In barely twenty years, living together without being married has gone from being frowned upon and virtually unheard of to being socially acceptable and commonplace. Many people choose to live together because they want to avoid the rules of marriage and thus, as they see it, make their lives less complicated. The irony is they often end up making life more complicated.

Married relationships are governed by the *Family Law Act* which applies throughout Australia. De facto relationships are governed by state law and may be different depending on which state you live in. It is only in the last fifteen or so years that any state has recognised to any significant degree that de facto relationships exist and that partners might require some protection from the law.

Queensland and Western Australia still don't have specific de facto relationships legislation. New South Wales, Victoria, South Australia and the two federal territories all have a de facto relationships Act, which deals mainly with property rights on separation. There are other more general laws, however, in all states, which for the most part treat de facto relationships in the same way as married relationships. Some examples are those relating to superannuation, workers compensation and social security. As a result, if your de facto spouse is killed in a workplace accident and has not made a will you may have the right to workers compensation but no right to a share in the estate.

To make matters even more difficult, there are two ways in which laws are made: by acts of parliament (statute law) and as a result of court decisions (common law). Even where there are no parliament-made laws dealing with de facto relationships, increasingly the courts are tending to reflect social reality and to recognise rights and obligations that once were non-existent. Consequently, even if, on the face of it, your rights as a de facto spouse seem limited, you should get legal advice as there may be action you can take.

One of the problems legislators and the courts have in deciding disputes between de facto couples is trying to balance what is fair and equitable with the need to avoid imposing values on people who have chosen not to marry precisely because they wish to avoid the obligations marriage entails. In 1986, one judge ruling on the then relatively new NSW *De Facto Relationships Act* put it thus:

> When parties enter into a marriage they do so consciously, knowing that they are entering into a voluntary union...for life and that there are obligations, both moral and legal, with respect to each other and their property. Many people in our society deliberately choose not to enter into that marriage relationship. Some do it because they value marriage so highly they do not wish, at least initially, to take on the full responsibilities of that state. Others deliberately do not do it because they have already had an unfortunate experience with marriage. To construe this Act so that parties who have deliberately refused to enter marriage are to be deemed for all purposes as if they had gone through the ceremony of marriage completely defeats these common intentions.

For the most part, both statute law and common law relate only to heterosexual relationships. In recent years, however, court decisions and even some statutes are conferring rights and obligations as a result of homosexual relationships (see Chapter Three, *Same-sex relationships*).

De factos defined

De facto is simply a Latin term meaning 'in fact'. It can be used in many ways, but traditionally it has referred to people who live together as if they were married even though they have not gone through a marriage ceremony. Of course, relationships of this kind range from cohabitation for a month or so, in what may be little more than a casual liaison, to stable relationships that last a lifetime. One of the difficulties legislators have encountered is defining when living together reaches a point of conferring legal rights and obligations.

The words used in the various Acts are different but for the most part they mean that to assert legal rights you must have been living with your partner in a genuine domestic relationship which is like that of a married couple. Usually the relationship must have lasted for at least two years unless you have a child when there is no minimum period of cohabitation. Even as far as this definition is concerned, however, the piecemeal way the legislation has developed means not only that it may be different according to where you live, but also it may be different according to the particular situation you are in—for example, whether you are claiming compensation if your partner is killed in an accident at work or making a claim on the estate if your partner dies without a will.

Acquiring property

Once you decide to acquire property together, it is important to decide how you want to do it as it is likely to have far-reaching ramifications. There are two ways to purchase property jointly, as joint tenants or as tenants-in-common.

Joint tenancy is usually preferable since it gives both partners ownership and passes automatically to the surviving partner if the other partner dies. However, the catch is that, since you own it equally, you also have an equal obligation to pay for it and if your partner defaults on the mortgage payments you can be held responsible. This may not seem to be a problem if you are in a good job and earning a reasonable wage, but if you lose your job or cease work to have a baby, you may not be able to take over the payments. Similarly, if your partner moves out and defaults on the payments you may have to meet them. Of course, the property can be sold but mortgagee sales don't always realise the full value—the lender is only interested in recouping the amount of the loan.

If you buy a home or block of land as tenants-in-common, you and your spouse have separate and identifiable shares in the property. The shares can be in any proportion you agree on. For example, if your partner earns more than you and will be making bigger payments, you may agree that the home will be owned 60/40, or whatever is appropriate. The problem with this form of ownership is that each partner is free to leave their share to whomever they choose in their will—so if your partner dies, you might find yourself with your partner's child as co-owner of your home. Each tenant-in-common is also free to sell their share, without the consent of the other tenant-in-common—although of course they have to find a buyer who is prepared to take on ownership with the remaining tenant-in-common. Think about home ownership carefully and get good legal advice.

You pay the mortgage, I'll pay the living expenses: how not to organise your finances

One partner paying the mortgage and the other partner paying the day-to-day living expenses is a common arrangement in de facto relationships. It often seems a logical and fair way to go, especially if the weekly outlays are roughly equivalent. There is only one possible piece of advice as to whether you should enter into such an arrangement. Don't!

If you are in a de facto relationship, who paid for the property is likely to be more important than if you are married, because in marriage all property acquired during the marriage is considered to be family property, irrespective of who paid for it, and in dividing the property what matters is what is fair in the circumstances. Some de facto relationship laws do now say that non-financial contributions to the relationship, such as looking after the home and family, should be taken into account in property settlements as well as financial contributions, but this is not the case in all states. In any event, it tends to be interpreted more narrowly than in the case of married relationships.

If you can prove you contributed to the mortgage payments or paid for improvements you will possibly have some claim to your home, even if it isn't in your name. But if you paid for the cornflakes and all those dinners at the local restaurant when you were disinclined to cook, while your partner paid off your love nest, guess who is more likely to end up with the love nest? Not you!

If you contribute to paying off the home even indirectly by meeting other expenses, at least make sure that you are named as an owner. It should be clearly agreed what share you each have, either 50/50 or whatever percentage is appropriate. Even estranged partners often agree that they are each entitled to some share of the home they have been living in—the dispute is usually, what share? Whoever has legal ownership starts a long way ahead.

If the relationship breaks down and you can establish that, even though your partner paid for the home, it was intended to be joint property, then you may have a stronger claim to a half share. But you need some supporting evidence. What are you going to produce? Have you kept all the grocery bills? Whatever you may have agreed in happier times over all those wonderful candlelit dinners can be hard to prove if your partner denies it.

You can only make a property claim if your partner is still alive. So, for example, if the home isn't in your name and your partner dies in a road accident without leaving a will, you can't ask the court to transfer the home to you, even if you contributed to the payments. You may have a claim on the estate, especially if you were dependent on your partner, but clearly that involves expensive legal fees and will take time to resolve.

See also Chapter Seven, *Ending a de facto relationship.*

Rented accommodation

If you rent an apartment or home, you need to decide if the lease will be in one name or both names. If it is in one partner's name, only that partner is responsible for the rent. If it is in both your names, you are each what is called 'jointly and severally liable' for the rent. This means that either of you can be called on to pay all the rent. If your partner decamps owing several months' rent, you can be made to pay it. You would have the right to sue your partner to get their share of the rent back but, although you might win the court case, you might not have much chance of actually getting the money if they don't have much or can't be found.

If there is any damage to the premises, if the lease is in joint names, either one of you can be responsible for paying for all the damage.

Financial agreements

One way the legislators have tried to overcome the difficulty of interfering with your freedom not to marry because you deliberately choose not to take on the rights and obligations imposed by marriage is to introduce financial agreements by which you can specifically state what the arrangements will be if you separate. These agreements usually have more legal force than agreements made before marriage. The agreements have different names in different states; for example, in New South Wales they are called cohabitation agreements and in the Australian Capital Territory they are called domestic relationship agreements. Although Western Australia doesn't have specific de facto relationships legislation, if you have a child there is some scope to make a financial agreement covering what will happen to property if you separate. The New South Wales law is the most established and that is what is dealt with here—check the detail if you live somewhere else.

A cohabitation agreement can be made before or after you start living together. It can deal with anything, including the sharing of domestic tasks, although most agreements are limited to financial matters. Some of the things an agreement might deal with are:

- how you will organise your ongoing living expenses;
- whether you will pool all or some of your wages or keep them separate;
- what will happen if one of you becomes pregnant;
- what will happen if one of you loses your job;
- how any property will be owned or leased;
- who will pay the mortgage;
- what rights to superannuation you each have, even if the policy is owned by only one of you;
- how property will be divided if the relationship ends;
- what will happen to the agreement if you decide to marry.

If you make an agreement because you think the relationship might end it is called a separation agreement. If the relationship hasn't ended after three months, then the agreement automatically becomes a cohabitation agreement.

For a cohabitation agreement to stand up in court, it must be in writing and signed by both of you. As well, there must be a certificate from a solicitor saying that each of you has received independent legal advice. As part of that advice, you must be told about your right to apply to the court for the agreement to be changed, whether or not it is financially or otherwise advantageous for you to enter into the agreement, whether it is prudent for you to enter into the agreement, and whether the agreement is fair and reasonable taking into account the circumstances at the time and any reasonably foreseeable circumstances.

If all these conditions are met, in most circumstances the court can't change the agreement. However, if even one of the conditions is not met, the court can make property and maintenance orders as if there had been no agreement. In this case, the court may take the agreement into account as an indication of what you wanted but it can nevertheless make whatever orders it thinks are appropriate.

In certain circumstances, the court can set aside a cohabitation agreement even if all the conditions have been met. This might happen if the court considers that the agreement is unjust, or if one of you was forced into signing it by violence or a threat of violence, or you didn't fully understand the agreement or you were in an unequal bargaining position. The court may also set aside an agreement where circumstances have changed so much since it was signed that it would lead to serious injustice if the agreement were enforced. An example of this might be if you had agreed that neither of you would ever claim maintenance from the other but, by the time you separated, you were so fully occupied looking after your children that it would be seriously unjust for you not to receive maintenance.

In Victoria, financial agreements of this kind are not necessarily binding although the law states that the judge must take an agreement into account. In the Northern Territory the requirement for independent legal advice before the agreement is signed is less stringent, but the court has more discretion to vary the agreement. In South Australia it is only necessary for a lawyer to be given 'apparently credible assurances' that you were not acting under coercion or undue influence.

If an agreement provides for the transfer of property on the death of your partner, that can be enforced against the estate. Periodic maintenance, however, ceases unless the agreement provides otherwise.

Children

The responsibility of both parents for their children is the same whether you are married or unmarried. If you separate, arrangements for the children are dealt with under the *Family Law Act* (there are some differences in Western Australia) which applies the same principles for all children—the best interests of the child are the most important consideration. Child support under the Child Support Scheme must be paid for all children whether you are married or unmarried.

Rights of unmarried fathers

Until relatively recently, although unmarried fathers had an obligation to support their children, they had few legal rights regarding them. Now, in the Family Court, both married and unmarried fathers are treated equally. Even in the state courts, where a child is born in a long-term de facto relationship it is unlikely that the father will be treated very differently because he and the mother did not marry. However, the situation may be different where a child is the result of a casual liaison. In particular, an unmarried father's consent may not always be necessary if the child is to be adopted, although this is changing (see also Chapter Four, *Having a baby*). A father, unmarried or married, cannot usually prevent the mother from having an abortion (see Chapter Ten, *Sex*).

If a child is given the father's surname at birth, the father's consent is normally required before the name can be changed—for example, if the mother later marries someone other than the father. However, the court may waive consent if the father plays no part in the child's life.

Grandparents and ex-nuptial children

It is often a source of sadness for grandparents that they rarely if ever see a grandchild fathered by a son as a result of a brief ex-nuptial relationship. Under the *Family Law Act*, grandparents now have the right to apply to the court for orders enabling them to see a grandchild, although such applications are not common. Probably part of the reason is that an order is hard to enforce if the mother refuses to comply with it. The only sanctions the court has are to fine the mother or send her to prison and it is unlikely that either option would be in the best interests of the child. But even if a matter doesn't reach the court, the fact that there is a legal right gives weight to a grandparent's wish to have contact with a grandchild.

Workers compensation

Throughout Australia, if your partner is injured or killed at work, as a de facto spouse you have the same rights as a married spouse. The amount of compensation may vary according to your level of dependence on your partner. For example, if you are earning a good income the compensation may be less than if you are a full-time homemaker.

Criminal injuries compensation

Criminal injuries compensation exists to compensate victims who have been injured as a result of crime. If the victim is killed, compensation may be payable to their dependants. It is only necessary to prove that you are a dependant, not whether you are married or in a de facto relationship. Compensation is normally payable to a maximum amount, depending on the state, but usually about $50 000.

In some instances you may be entitled to compensation if you can establish that you are a 'secondary victim'. This applies if you suffered some injury (e.g. nervous shock) as a direct result of witnessing or becoming aware in some other way of the injury to the primary victim.

Superannuation

It is generally now not permissible by law for a superannuation fund to give benefits or a higher level of benefits upon a member's death or incapacity to those members in a formal married relationship than to those in a de facto relationship. However, some longstanding funds that existed before superannuation funds were subject to antidiscrimination laws may still make a distinction between married and unmarried spouses. Your position may depend on the date of the fund and how long your partner has been a member.

Discrimination

Discrimination means treating you unfairly because you belong to a particular group or have a particular characteristic. It is against the law to discriminate against someone because of their marital status. If you are a victim of discrimination because you are in a de facto relationship, you should complain to the antidiscrimination office in your state. Some organisations are exempt from antidiscrimination legislation and it may be possible for a religion-based private school, for example, to refuse to employ you if their philosophy disapproves of such relationships. Similarly, if a job involves working in a person's residence they may refuse to employ you on the basis that you are living in a de facto relationship.

Employers are sometimes allowed to insist that a job can only be done by a 'married couple'. The extent to which a de facto couple is covered by the term 'married couple' is sometimes open to question depending on the circumstances and the state. Depending on the state, small businesses with fewer than five employees may also be exempt from the antidiscrimination laws.

Insurance providers are able to discriminate between people on the grounds of gender, disability and age. However, they may not discriminate on the basis of de facto marital status.

If your partner dies

If your partner dies, it is especially important for them to have a will as your right to make a claim on their estate may be very different from your right to claim if you were married. If there is no will, a married spouse is the first person with a claim on the estate, but many state intestacy laws do not include a de facto spouse among those people who are entitled to share the estate.

De facto spouses, nevertheless, do have increasing rights to a partner's estate and if there is no will or if you are inadequately provided for in your partner's will you should get legal advice, especially if you were dependent on your partner. Even in states where de facto partners have few rights to an estate *per se*, the courts are tending to view claims of this kind more sympathetically than might once have been the case. Usually there is a minimum period of living together before any rights to a partner's estate exist, for example, two years. However, if you have a child of the relationship there is usually no minimum period.

In some circumstances, you may have a right to claim on a de facto partner's estate even if the relationship has ended before your partner's death. Also, in some circumstances, even if your partner was still married to someone else, you may take the place of the surviving legal spouse so far as the estate is concerned—for example, if your partner and their spouse had never formally divorced but you had been living together for some time.

chapter two

LOVE AND MARRIAGE

Marriage is essentially a contract and a hundred years ago the law was full of the rights and obligations entailed in that contract—the rights usually applying to the husband and the obligations usually applying to the wife. Gradually these rights and obligations have at least been diluted and many have disappeared, so that any remaining rights and obligations are mutual, with no distinction on the basis of gender. Similarly, in the past, when a couple married, the wife promised to 'love, honour, and obey' her husband. Today, even in traditional religious ceremonies, the promise to obey is usually omitted.

As living together has lost its stigma and become socially acceptable more and more couples are asking—why get married? Even twenty years ago the answer would have been easy. Until the 1980s, leaving aside the question of personal commitment, being married meant that there were tax advantages, social security advantages, inheritance advantages and injury compensation advantages that did not apply to couples who simply lived together. Today, however, in many situations the test is simply whether a spouse, de facto or married, is dependent on the other spouse. Nevertheless, most people still go along with the notion that marriage is the preferred state for two people who want to live together and there are many other circumstances in which married couples have more rights and protection from the law, in relation to each other, than unmarried couples.

Marriage is also generally regarded as the most suitable institution for bringing up children. From a legal point of view, although there is no longer any distinction between the rights of children born within a marriage and children born outside a marriage, it is sometimes easier for children born within a marriage to establish who their parents are and so to assert their rights. It is also sometimes easier for a father to establish rights *vis-à-vis* a child if the father is married to the mother.

Age at which you can marry

You must be at least sixteen before you can legally marry.

If you are sixteen or seventeen, you can get married if you have the consent of your parents and/or the court, *and* your intended spouse is at least eighteen. In other words, if you are both under eighteen you may not marry. If one of you is at least eighteen and the other is over sixteen, you can marry if your parents and the court agree to the marriage. However, if your parents will not consent, you can ask the court for permission and if this is granted you can then marry without your parents' consent. The court will have to be persuaded that you are mature enough and that very special circumstances exist before it will grant permission—pregnancy alone is not usually considered a sufficiently good reason for the court to agree to a marriage.

Once you turn eighteen, it is a matter for you if you wish to marry and you do not need anyone else's consent.

> Melanie was sixteen and Shane was twenty-one and they had been going out together for four years. Although they had been living together for six months they had never had sex because their religious convictions said that intercourse before marriage was a sin. They applied to the court which granted them special permission to marry.

If you lie about your age

It is difficult to lie successfully about your age in order to get married because normally a birth certificate is required. However, if you were to lie and perhaps forge the documents, your marriage would not be valid if you were under sixteen. If you were over sixteen your marriage would be valid but you could be prosecuted for deceiving the authorities.

Who can't you marry?

You are not allowed to marry certain close relatives. These are:

- your parents
- your grandparents
- your brothers and sisters (including half-brothers and half-sisters).

This includes people who are related in these ways by adoption. It does not, however, include step relationships and, for example, a stepbrother and sister are legally able to marry. There is obviously some inconsistency in this. The main reason people related closely by blood may not marry is because the increased risk of passing on genetic disease to their children is generally considered not to be in society's best interests; and yet first cousins can marry whereas people who are related by adoption and not by blood cannot. Adopted people not only may not marry their (prohibited) adopted relatives, they may not marry their blood relatives who come into the prohibited categories either.

A valid marriage

A marriage will be a valid marriage only if:

- neither of you is already married to someone else;
- you are of the opposite sex;
- neither of you is under duress;
- neither of you is misled as to the identity of the person you are marrying or the nature of the ceremony;
- both of you understand fully what you are doing.

If one party to a marriage is already married, it is bigamy; not only will the marriage not be valid, the person concerned may be prosecuted. In practice, prosecution is rare if the bigamy is unintentional; for example, a person believes that a divorce has taken place in another country.

If one party is forced to marry, then the marriage will not be valid. While force does not necessarily mean actual physical force but can include threats of physical harm, it must be real duress, not just pressure because you are, for example, pregnant, or you want to please your parents.

At present, homosexual marriages are not valid in the eyes of the law, although some homosexuals go through a ceremony, possibly conducted in a church or by a minister of religion, which, for them, is the equivalent of a marriage commitment.

Notice of intention to marry

You must give the marriage celebrant notice of your intention to marry at least one month and not more than six months before the marriage is to take place. Under some circumstances, the waiting period of one month can be shortened—but you need to have a very good reason for this to be done. You will have to fill out a Notice of Intention to Marry and supply a copy of your birth certificate and, if you are divorced or widowed, a copy of the divorce decree or death certificate of your former spouse. If you are under the marrying age, you will need the required consents.

Who can perform the marriage ceremony?

The marriage ceremony must be performed by an authorised person. This includes ministers of recognised religions, registrars and deputy registrars of births, deaths and marriages, and civil marriage celebrants appointed by the federal attorney general. Some diplomatic and consular officials can perform a marriage, provided the official is the same nationality as one of the couple.

The romantic notion of being married at sea by the captain of a ship doesn't have much basis in law. There are some circumstances in which a marriage performed by a ship's captain might be valid but it depends on which laws apply—and that depends on which waters the ship is sailing in. In general, such a marriage would not be valid if either party was an Australian citizen and therefore covered by Australian law.

The marriage ceremony

There are four recognised marriage ceremonies in Australia:

- *civil ceremony*: performed by an authorised celebrant, this can take place in any setting, from a garden to a mountain; marriage celebrants are listed in the phone book;
- *registry marriage*: performed by a registry official at the Registry for Births, Deaths and Marriages;

- *religious ceremony:* performed by a minister of religion, usually in a church and incorporated in a religious service;
- *foreign marriage*: performed by an authorised consular or diplomatic official within Australia but according to the law of the relevant country.

Legally, the marriage ceremony does not have to follow any particular form and you are free to have a ceremony that is meaningful for you or traditional to the church in which you are marrying. However, whatever the ceremony consists of, you must exchange vows, in the presence of the celebrant, that say something like: 'I (full name) take you (full name) to be my lawful wedded wife/husband'.

The wedding ring

It is customary for the man to give the woman a wedding ring as part of the ceremony. Often, the woman gives the man a ring as well. This is purely a matter of convention and there is no legal requirement for it to happen.

Overseas marriages

A marriage that takes place overseas between non-Australian citizens is normally regarded as valid in Australia, if it is valid in the country in which it was performed. However, polygamous marriages are not valid in Australia, regardless of their status in another country. If either of you is an Australian citizen, then Australian marriage requirements must be complied with.

Foreign marriages in Australia

A marriage performed in Australia according to the laws of another country will be regarded as valid if it is carried out before a diplomatic or consular official of the country concerned. However, the marriage will not be valid if the two people who marry are related in one of the ways prohibited by Australian law.

What's your name?

Although traditionally a woman has taken her husband's name on marriage there is no legal compulsion to do this and increasingly women keep their single name. Some women use their single name for business purposes and their married name socially. Some women combine their single name with their married name, for example, Ann White-Black. If you separate or divorce, you can revert to your single name or continue to use your married name.

What's his, what's yours?

Ownership of property you bring to the marriage remains yours. For example, if you have a family heirloom, it remains yours to do what you wish with, including giving it away or leaving it to whomever you please in your will. Similarly with any property or other assets which you either bring to the marriage or buy yourself while you are married. If you own or buy jewellery or an investment property you can do whatever you like with it, including selling it without reference to your spouse, or giving it to your children.

Arguments about property ownership are rare while the marriage lasts. It isn't very likely that you and your spouse will debate who owns the silver if you have an amicable relationship. Disputes normally only arise when the marriage looks like ending and, then, the question of individual ownership may be looked at differently (see Chapter Six, *Ending a marriage*).

Pre-nuptial agreements

Before marrying some couples make a pre-nuptial agreement setting out the financial arrangements, including how assets will be divided if the marriage breaks down. Making a pre-nuptial agreement is still not common in Australia but, especially if the assets of one or both parties are considerable, some couples see such an agreement as a way of avoiding disputes in the event of a later break-up. The government has said that it proposes to amend the law so that pre-nuptial agreements will be binding. At the time of writing, however, a pre-nuptial agreement has little legal standing and, if you divorce, you are expected to divide the assets according to what is fair, taking into account the circumstances that exist at the time. Currently, the main value of a pre-nuptial agreement is probably that it makes you think carefully about the issues.

A pre-nuptial agreement would certainly not be enforced if it disadvantaged one of you, or if one of you did not fully understand the implications at the time of signing, or if circumstances had changed since you signed it—for example, a child had been born and the agreement did not take this into account.

A pre-nuptial agreement may carry more weight if the marriage does not last very long. It provides a guide to what you both intended if a court is asked to adjudicate. If you do enter into a pre-nuptial agreement, make sure you each get proper advice. Women in particular tend to accept the major responsibility for making the relationship work and sometimes do things that are not in their best interests. A properly drawn agreement will be flexible enough to take account of changing circumstances—for example, by ensuring that the assets are divided proportionately in the event that the marriage breaks down, rather than specifying a particular amount.

> One celebrated pre-nuptial agreement in America was that entered into by the actor, Joan Collins, and her husband, Peter Holm, during the 1980s. When they separated after thirteen months of marriage, Holm asked for a settlement of $2.8 million, which was half of the $5.6 million Collins had earned during the period of the marriage and which he would have been entitled to under Californian law. However, the court held that the pre-nuptial agreement the couple had signed was valid. This limited Holm's settlement to twenty per cent of any income earned during the marriage.

Marriage and sex

An exclusive sexual relationship is normally considered to be part of marriage. Until about twenty-five years ago marriage was seen as conferring a right to exclusive sex and there were sanctions if one or other party didn't live up to their obligations in this regard. Non-consummation or the failure to have an ongoing sexual relationship was grounds for divorce. Adultery was grounds for divorce. There was no such thing as 'rape' within marriage because a man who forcibly had sex with his wife was simply asserting 'his rights'. The court could make an order that a spouse who left the marriage or, indeed, who refused to have sex should resume 'cohabitation'. If a wife refused to move with her husband, for example, because he had been transferred interstate, he could sue for divorce on the ground of 'constructive desertion'.

Today there is no legal sanction that can be imposed on the ground that a sexual relationship no longer exists, or that the other spouse has an affair. If a spouse does not wish to continue in a marriage where there is no sex, or where the other spouse commits adultery, they simply separate and seek a divorce after twelve months on the basis that the marriage has irretrievably broken down.

Right to support

In a practical sense, the only right that marriage confers today and which can be enforced to some extent is the right of each spouse to be supported by the other. If your spouse earns an income and you do not, you must be provided with a home, food and reasonable clothing or you can seek a court order. However, you can't force your spouse to get a job in order to support you. The court will not normally make an order saying that someone has to obtain employment—and even if it did, it would be impossible to enforce. If someone refused to comply with such an order, they could only be fined or sent to jail and neither sanction would remedy the situation. If your spouse's income is not enough to support you, you will have to support yourself.

If you both work there is no law that says you must both contribute to the household expenses; rather it is considered a matter for you to work out between yourselves.

Neither of you has the right to know what the other spouse earns, but if an application for support is made each spouse's income must usually be revealed to the court.

What about the housework?

In this time of sexual equality, when each spouse may work and share the financial responsibility of running a home, is there any way that both spouses can be compelled to share the housework? Unfortunately, no! Legally, there is nothing you can do to make sure that the housekeeping chores are divided fairly. It may be possible to work out a plan in a pre-nuptial agreement—but it seems unlikely that any sanctions would be upheld. Generally the courts don't like interfering in what might be called 'family matters' that do not involve basic support.

Social rights

All of us have rights in relation to the society in which we live and you don't relinquish these by marrying. Apart from the right to own property in your own name, you can enter into contracts, obtain credit, carry on business activities and keep your own earnings (subject to the other spouse's right of support).

Discrimination and marriage

Thirty years ago married women were barely tolerated in the workforce. It was frequently asserted that: 'When a woman falls in love, she loses interest in the job, when a man falls in love, he works twice as hard!' Women were rarely promoted because they 'will just get married and have a baby'. As a result women managers were almost non-existent. In the professions, such as law and accountancy, many firms refused to employ women 'as a matter of policy'.

Today marriage is one of the main grounds on which discrimination has been outlawed. It is unlawful for you to be denied a job, paid less, given less favourable treatment, denied promotion or dismissed because you are married. Discrimination is against the law whether it is direct and obvious, or indirect and subtle. Discrimination is also unlawful if it is unintentional; indeed, it often results from unconsciously held beliefs and attitudes. It is unacceptable for a potential employer to ask how you will fit in family responsibilities with your job, or if you intend to have children.

You may not be denied educational or training opportunities on the basis of your marital status. In particular, it is discriminatory to refuse a woman access to training courses 'because she will get pregnant and the investment will be wasted'.

Sometimes finding a marriage partner has special implications under the antidiscrimination laws.

> A Melbourne woman, Mrs P, applied to the Anti-Discrimination Tribunal for an exemption from the *Equal Opportunity Act* so that she could operate a dating agency exclusively for Jewish people. Her application was originally refused but, subsequently, after new evidence was presented, the tribunal granted the application saying that it was satisfied that the dating service would allow Jews an equal opportunity to find a life partner. The tribunal made it clear that this should not be regarded as a precedent and that any other applications of this kind would be decided on the evidence.

Medical treatment

Medical treatment is a question for you alone and you do not have to seek permission from or even refer to your spouse. This applies to abortion, contraception and anything that may affect your reproductive processes. For example, a woman does not need her husband's consent to have a hysterectomy or to have her tubes tied, nor does a man need his wife's consent for a vasectomy.

Your will

Because of the right of support each spouse is entitled to be provided for in the other spouse's will. A will is automatically revoked on marriage, unless it is made in a particular way, so you must normally make a new will when you marry. You don't have to discuss your will with your spouse or disclose what is in it. Nor do you have to make your spouse an executor, although many people choose to (see Chapter Thirteen, *Love and death*).

Your passport

If you change your name on marriage you can get a new passport without paying the fee again. If necessary (e.g. because you want to honeymoon overseas) you can get the passport before the wedding provided you undertake to surrender it if the marriage doesn't take place.

Taking legal action against your spouse

At one time, married couples were considered 'as one' and so taking legal action against a spouse was a tricky business since, from a legal point of view, it amounted to suing yourself. Such a spurious concept was discarded many years ago and now, by and large, if you can take legal action against anyone else, you can take it against your spouse. Most legal action against a spouse arises because of negligence, commonly in the case of a motor vehicle accident, when one spouse is the driver and the other is injured. The payout is normally covered by third party insurance.

Giving evidence against your spouse

The other situation in which you might have to tangle with your spouse in the courts is if you want or are asked to give evidence against them. In this case, there is a difference between the rules applying to your spouse and the rules applying to other people. In the case of other people, you can be required by means of a subpoena to give evidence against them, even if you don't wish to. This is not so in the case of your spouse. If you *want* to give evidence against your spouse, you can. However, if you are *asked* to give evidence against your spouse, you are entitled to refuse.

There is sometimes an exception to this in domestic violence cases when the spouse who has suffered the violence can be required to give evidence against the spouse who has perpetrated the violence (see Chapter Eleven, *Violence*).

Second time around

Today, one-third of marriages end in divorce and, since most divorcees remarry, many people marry two, three or even more times. The main area in which subsequent marriages impact is on the transfer of property by will. If there are children from a previous marriage you probably want to take them into account in your will and you may want to avoid your assets passing to stepchildren, especially if they have not grown up with you or will be well provided for by their own parent.

There are various arrangements you can make, ranging from outright bequests to putting the home and other assets in trust for use by your spouse during his or her lifetime, passing to your children on your spouse's death. There are advantages and disadvantages to all the options and you should get good advice, both as to what is most appropriate for your particular circumstances, and to avoid later disputes. The courts are full of challenges to a parent's will by children who feel that a later spouse has usurped their inheritance—a course of action that not only reduces your estate but may cause great distress and even hardship to your surviving spouse (see also Chapter Thirteen, *Love and death*).

chapter three

SAME-SEX RELATIONSHIPS

Until recently, in common with most countries in the world, male homosexuality was a crime in Australia. As a result of our British legal heritage, female homosexuality, or lesbianism, has never been a crime in this country—allegedly because Queen Victoria said, 'No woman would do such a thing.' Whether or not that is the reason, lesbians have been more or less ignored until recent times when more women have been prepared to come out publicly and admit their sexual orientation.

During the 1980s most states decriminalised homosexuality between consenting adults and a 1997 decision by the High Court put the matter beyond doubt.

Despite the fact that homosexuality is no longer an offence, in most states there are currently no specific laws that deal with same-sex relationships in the way that the *Marriage Act* and the various de facto relationships acts deal with heterosexual relationships. For a marriage to be legally valid, it must be between people of the opposite sex. Similarly, in those statutes in which a partner is given rights by virtue of a married or de facto relationship—for example, to compensation or to the other partner's estate—both those relationships are defined as being between people of the opposite sex.

Without some legislative recognition it is virtually impossible for same-sex partners to claim the same rights and responsibilities as heterosexual partners and, in general, same-sex partners face inequalities in superannuation, inheritance, property rights, access to IVF technology, organ donation in the event of the death of a partner, adoption, tax and employment benefits.

However, the situation is improving. In 1994, the Australian Capital Territory passed its groundbreaking *Domestic Relationships Act*. That Act was modelled on the NSW *De Facto Relationships Act* but, significantly, changed the wording from 'de facto' to 'domestic' and defined the relationships regulated by the Act as:

> A personal relationship (other than a legal marriage) between two adults in which one provides personal or financial commitment and support of a domestic nature for the material benefit of the other, and includes a de facto marriage.

Another more recent breakthrough has occurred in New South Wales, which in May 1999 passed the most liberal laws in Australia for same-sex couples, giving them the same property and inheritance rights as heterosexual couples. A new Wills Act in Victoria emphasises dependency as the main factor in inheritance rights rather than blood relationships. Legislation is before the Queensland parliament to recognise same-sex relationships under industrial relationships laws. Even where statutory recognition is still limited, there is some indication that the courts are viewing the existence of long-term, stable same-sex relationships as a ground on which various rights and obligations may be inferred. Anyone who wishes to assert what they consider to be a legal right in relation to a homosexual partner should get good legal advice.

The main recognition of homosexuality occurs in anti-discrimination and anti-vilification legislation and yet even these laws lead to some anomalous situations. Antidiscrimination laws generally prohibit discrimination on the basis of marital status. Accordingly, a person who has been discriminated against on the basis of marital status can lodge a complaint. However, people in same-sex relationships are excluded from the definition of marital status, since both married and de facto couples are invariably defined as being of opposite sexes. Consequently, a partner in a same-sex relationship is ineligible to lodge a complaint on this basis—however, they may be able to complain on the ground of discrimination based on sexual preference.

Setting up home together

If you plan to set up house with a same-sex partner, the best way to protect both of you if the relationship breaks down is to make a cohabitation agreement. The law may not specifically provide for same-sex cohabitation agreements but that doesn't mean you can't make one.

The agreement should cover what will happen to property you own or acquire during the relationship, whether there will be any obligations as to support if the relationship ends and what financial contribution each of you intends to make to the relationship. If there are children involved, you may wish to set out what the arrangements will be for them if either of you dies or the relationship ends. As with heterosexual relationships, the agreement will not be binding as far as children are concerned and in the event of a dispute the court will decide according to what is in the best interests of the children; however, an agreement provides an indication of what you would like and the court will usually take it into account.

Illness

Stories abound in the gay community of hospitals that refuse gay or lesbian access to a seriously ill same-sex partner. However, this is becoming less common. Similarly, while in theory a same-sex partner can't give consent as next of kin for an operation if the person concerned is unable to give consent personally, in practice many hospitals and doctors turn a blind eye and accept the partner's signature.

Death of a partner

Even more than in the case of the population at large, the golden rule for homosexual couples is to make a will. Except where the laws have been changed a same-sex partner has no automatic right of inheritance under the intestacy laws.

It may be possible to make a claim if the surviving partner can establish a level of dependency on the deceased. Dependency normally means financial dependency and not emotional dependency. However, it is now probably fair to say that where the parties were in a relationship and shared household responsibilities the court will take the view that each partner was dependent on the other. Nevertheless, the matter has to be argued and establishing the claim is clearly more difficult and expensive than if the deceased's wishes are clearly stated in a will.

> Arthur and Harry had lived together for twelve years, when Arthur suffered a fatal heart attack, aged forty-eight. He died without leaving a will. During their time together, Arthur took Harry on overseas trips and gave him expensive jewellery as gifts. Harry did not earn as much as Arthur and while Harry made financial contributions to the household, Arthur paid the rent and took overall responsibility for the finances. On his death, Arthur left an estate worth about $500 000, which included the

apartment where the two lived, furniture, savings and investments, superannuation and a one-third interest in his mother's estate (his mother had died six weeks earlier). Arthur's brothers informed Harry that they intended to sell the apartment giving him one-third of the purchase price. This was Harry's home and he was devastated. He took the matter to court, claiming he had been dependent on Arthur. The court awarded Harry the apartment worth $325 000, its contents valued at $18 000 and a $25 000 legacy. The judge said that he had not approached the matter 'in a way different from how one would approach a heterosexual relationship between a man and wife or a man and his de facto wife'.

Even if there is a will, where a partner has died of AIDS there have been instances of family members contesting the will on the grounds that the deceased did not know what he was doing as a result of AIDS dementia. Anyone in this situation should get a doctor's certificate to establish that they were sane at the time the will was made.

The executor of the will has the legal right and responsibility to make funeral arrangements and decide whether the body should be buried or cremated. If there is no will, the decision is made by the next of kin. Same-sex partners are not included in the definition of 'next of kin'. However, if there is no close relative, the person under whose roof the person died may make the necessary decisions and, of course, this may be the deceased's partner.

If there is a coroner's inquest into the death, a same-sex partner does not have an automatic right of appearance but must apply to the court for the right to appear and make submissions.

Partner's mental incapacity

Where a person becomes mentally incapable of making their own decisions, unless that person has made provision by giving an enduring power of attorney to a same-sex partner, the question will usually be decided by the guardianship authority. Generally, the law sets out who is appropriate to make decisions on the person's behalf. Under some circumstances, same-sex partners can be considered. A power of attorney does not cover medical treatment.

Property

When a relationship ends, heterosexual partners usually have some rights to property acquired during the relationship under either the *Family Law Act* or the various de facto relationships acts. Same-sex partners have no such rights. If a same-sex partner can establish that they have partly paid for the property, they may be able to make a successful claim in the Equity Court, but they would have little chance of persuading the court of any rights as a result of non-financial contribution to the relationship. If there is no written agreement as to what the partners intended and the property is in the name of only one partner, making a successful claim is not easy.

Same-sex partners do not have the exemption from stamp duty that heterosexual couples have when one partner buys the other out of jointly acquired property on the termination of a relationship.

Insurance and superannuation

Unless a homosexual partner is named as a beneficiary by the owner of an insurance or superannuation fund, it is often a matter for the trustees to exercise their discretion as to whether to meet a claim on the fund. Again, as community attitudes change, trustees are more likely to view same-sex partner claims sympathetically. But it is a good deal simpler for the survivor if the matter is put beyond doubt because they have been named in the original policy. Especially if there is a dispute over the will, trustees will often refuse to make any payment pending the resolution of the dispute. The beneficiaries to a superannuation or insurance policy can be changed at any time so, even if a person was not named at the time the fund was established, they can be named subsequently.

Compensation

For the most part same-sex partners do not have an automatic right to compensation under the various laws that provide for this. In the case of workers compensation, for example, heterosexual de facto partners can often claim compensation. Homosexual partners have to incur the expense of a court case to establish similar rights. An exception is New South Wales which now gives workers compensation rights to 'unrelated adult persons' who live together in a genuine, continuing relationship where there is mutual commitment.

Social security

For the most part no distinction is made between homosexual and heterosexual claimants in terms of social security entitlements. In particular, people who are unable to work due to illness, including AIDS, may be eligible for the Sickness Allowance and Disability Support Pension, depending on the degree of incapacity. A person caring full-time at home for someone who is ill may be eligible for the Carer Pension or the Domiciliary Nursing Care Benefit.

Parenting orders

Where a same-sex parent is disputing with the other parent arrangements for a child of a previous relationship, the Family Court will decide according to the best interests of the child. A parent's homosexuality will be a factor to be considered in deciding what is in the child's best interests, but there is no legal reason why a lesbian or gay parent cannot be granted a residence or contact order and the Family Court has not infrequently done so. In one recent case, a gay man was granted custody of his son in a case that was heard in a local court. The magistrate said that the father of the child 'could provide an affectionate, stable and good family household, whereas his ex-wife's household was stressed and crisis-ridden, with hysteria a not infrequently prevailing mood'.

Co-parents

A same-sex partner who has agreed to share in the raising of a child with the biological parent does not have any legally recognised responsibilities or rights in relation to that child. If the relationship ends, as with heterosexual relationships, it is best for all concerned if the arrangements for any children can be mutually agreed. However, if there is a dispute, parenting orders can be made with regard to any person 'concerned with the care, welfare or development of the child' and this would normally include a person with whom the child had been living, especially if a close relationship had developed. As with any matter concerning children, the decision will be made with the best interests of the child as the paramount consideration.

In one case, even though the *Child Support Act* does not deal with co-parents, a woman was ordered by the court to pay child support for the children born by artificial insemination to her lesbian partner of eight years.

Adoption

Adoption by same-sex couples is not provided for in the legislation. However, single applicants are sometimes able to adopt, usually a child with special needs. If you are in a same-sex relationship you need to establish that special circumstances exist before you can adopt your partner's child.

Reproductive technology

In some states, such as Victoria, in-vitro fertilisation and other reproductive technology may only be provided to married couples. States such as New South Wales don't have a specific prohibition that denies fertility treatment to same-sex couples and, in theory, fertility clinics are bound by the antidiscrimination laws. However, there is anecdotal evidence that clinics are selective in whom they will accept—for example, they may say to a lesbian that no donor sperm is available.

See also Chapter Four, *Having a baby*.

Tax

Same-sex couples are not entitled to the various tax benefits available to heterosexual couples because the definition of 'spouse' in the legislation encompasses only married or de facto spouses. Similarly, the legislation dealing with the Medicare levy, which is higher if the taxpayer has a dependent spouse, does not include a same-sex partner in its definition of 'dependent spouse'.

Migration to Australia

One of the grounds on which permanent visas to Australia are granted is that the applicant lives in an 'interdependent' relationship with an Australian citizen. This is defined as having a mutual commitment to a shared life to the exclusion of any other interdependent relationships, such as with a married or de facto spouse. The factors that the immigration authorities must consider in making a judgment are much the same as the factors to be considered in determining whether a heterosexual relationship exists.

Discrimination

Antidiscrimination is the area where same-sex relationships are most recognised by the legal system. Federal law, and that of many states (not Queensland, Western Australia or Tasmania), prohibits discrimination on the basis of a person's sexual preference. If you consider you are being discriminated against because you are homosexual, you can complain to the antidiscrimination authority in your state. The law applies to most aspects of life; for example, same-sex couples have the same rights as anyone else to rent a flat. However, most discrimination complaints relate to the workplace.

> In his job as a cook, Bill was systematically taunted and harassed about his sexuality by his boss, Simone, as a result of which he eventually resigned. Simone referred to Bill as a 'poofter, a poo jabber and a faggot', she issued him with trousers too small in a deliberate attempt to humiliate him and called him Wilhelmina, despite his objections to his treatment. Simone also locked Bill in a cupboard, telling him he was 'going back in the closet', and took no action against workers who drew demeaning caricatures

of him. The organisation that employed Bill and Simone was fined $5000 and Bill was awarded $3000 compensation.

Vilification

Increasingly, homosexual, transgender and HIV/AIDS vilification is prohibited by law. The vilification laws cover any public act that could encourage hatred, serious contempt or severe ridicule because of a person's homosexuality (male or female); a person's HIV or AIDS status; a person's transgender identity.

Where they exist, the antivilification laws are still relatively new but it seems likely they will cover speeches, taunts, verbal abuse, slogans, badges and other symbols, publications of various kinds, posters, stickers and graffiti. The laws don't prohibit such things as genuine academic or literary statements or fair media reporting.

part two

Having children

chapter four

HAVING A BABY

It may seem strange to think of the law in relation to something as natural as having a baby. But numerous medical tests and procedures are normally involved in pregnancy and birth and along with these go expectations of competence and skill on the part of the doctor. If those attributes are lacking, it may have legal implications. If you adopt a child or have a child using reproductive technology the law assumes even greater importance.

Natural pregnancies

Birthing options

Most women have their baby in hospital under the care of a doctor. However, you may choose to have the baby at home assisted by a midwife. Some hospitals have birthing centres which are more relaxed and informal than a traditional delivery ward. The choice is yours.

Standard of care

A doctor treating you when you are pregnant must exercise the standard of care and skill normally expected of an average practitioner of that type. For example, a specialist obstetrician is normally expected to exercise to a higher standard of care and skill than a general practitioner. If something goes wrong as a result of the doctor not meeting this standard of care, you have the right to take action for negligence. This applies to any tests or procedures carried out during the pregnancy, and while the child is being born.

Similarly, midwives must exercise a reasonable standard of care, having regard to their qualifications. A midwife who fails to do this may be guilty of negligence or, in some cases, professional misconduct. Midwives must be qualified and registered by the Australian College of Midwives and most are highly competent.

Of course, it is possible for things to go wrong in pregnancy and childbirth for any number of reasons not connected with the health worker's negligence. Giving birth to a less than perfect child is such a devastating experience for most people that they tend to look for someone to blame. There is evidence that many medical practitioners now are reluctant to become specialist obstetricians because of the high likelihood of being sued. Apart from the personal cost of litigation to the doctor, insurance premiums for these specialties are set at many thousands of dollars annually and that, of course, is reflected in the fees that are charged.

Consent

You must give informed consent before any test or procedure can be carried out. This means that you must be told of any risks involved, in a way that you can understand, so that you can make up your own mind whether to go ahead. The doctor may have an excuse for not warning you of what can go wrong if they have a reasonable view that it might damage your mental or physical health—but this argument would be hard to sustain in a normal pregnancy.

Similarly, you are entitled to know what are the likely effects on your child of any drugs prescribed during your pregnancy and to make an informed choice as to whether to take them, in light of the fact that many drugs can have a harmful effect on the foetus.

Abnormalities

If tests show up an abnormality in the foetus, some women may wish to consider an abortion. Other women decide to go ahead with the pregnancy regardless of the outcome. The decision is entirely a matter for you and perhaps your partner. While you may wish to seek counselling, you should not allow yourself to be pressured either way.

One of the very difficult and sad questions relates to the keeping alive of new-born babies who are profoundly handicapped and who have no chance of growing up to lead a normal life. New techniques mean that children who would once have died soon after birth can now be kept alive, and parents may be faced with an agonising decision as to whether or not to consent to treatment for their baby. It is a question that the law has not adequately come to terms with. In some cases, life-preserving treatment is withdrawn, normally after discussion with the parents, but the legal position is far from clear.

> In Victoria in 1986, a baby was born suffering from spina bifida. The child's grandfather asked the court to order that the hospital where the baby was born should take all steps to preserve the child's life. It was alleged that the baby had been sedated and denied nourishment for two or three days.
>
> The baby was made a ward of the court and the hospital was

ordered to take all steps to keep the baby alive. The judge said that no parent, doctor or court had any power to determine that the life of any child, however disabled, would be deliberately taken from it.

In another case:

A child who was born suffering from Down syndrome and an intestinal blockage required an operation to relieve the obstruction if she was to live more than a few days. If the operation were performed, the child might die within a few months but it was probable that her life expectancy would be twenty or thirty years. Her parents decided that it would be kinder to allow her to die and refused consent to the operation. The local authority made the child a ward of the court and sought an order that the operation be performed. The judge held that the parents' wishes should be respected and refused to make the order. The local authority appealed. The appeal court said that the question at issue was the best interests of the child and not whether the wishes of the parents should be respected. Since the effect of the operation might be that the child would have the normal lifespan of a Down syndrome person and since it had not been demonstrated that the life of such a person was so intolerable that the child should be condemned to die, the court ordered that the operation be performed.

Access to medical records

In the event of a dispute with your doctor, your right to see your medical records is not entirely clear. Legally, records kept by the doctor belong to the doctor and you have no right to see them if the doctor refuses a request. Where the records are relevant to legal action, the court may order that the records be made available for inspection and copying. Given that it is your body, it may seem strange that you can't see what notes the doctor has made, but doctors argue that they are entitled to keep private notes for their own purposes which won't necessarily be made available to the patient.

Many hospitals have policy guidelines stating that patients may ask the doctor in charge of their case for access to their medical file.

Adopting a child

You can only adopt a child through the state adoption department or an approved private agency. It is an offence to arrange an adoption directly with another couple. It is also an offence to offer or accept money or any other incentive in relation to adoption.

Even if relatives are adopting a child, the adoption must go through the proper channels, although it is likely that the adoption will be approved, provided it is in the child's best interests.

Where natural parents are still alive, it is often considered desirable that they have contact with a child who has been adopted. It may be a condition of the adoption that a child is told who its natural parents are and given the opportunity to remain in contact with them. Generally, both the child and the natural parents have a right to information about each other unless either party has placed a veto on this.

If you want to adopt a child from overseas you must comply with Australian adoption laws, the adoption laws of the country in which the child was born and Australian immigration laws.

Once a child is adopted it has the same legal rights as a natural born child. In particular, the child has the right to be supported by its adoptive parents and the right to be provided for in an adoptive parent's estate. If parents do not make adequate provision for an adopted child in their will, the child can apply to the court for the will to be changed.

Reproductive technology

The ability of couples to have children when one or other partner is infertile is one of the most dramatic advances of modern medicine. In Australia, about one per cent of births result from fertility treatments. Techniques range from the relatively simple insertion of sperm from a donor male into the vagina of the woman whose partner is infertile to other more complicated methods in which egg and sperm are brought together outside the body.

Despite numerous enquiries into the ethical and legal implications of the various techniques, this is an area where technology has definitely outstripped the law. Some of the issues that arise relate to the child's right to know its biological parentage, responsibility for the support of the child, to whom should the new technology be available and what happens if there is a dispute over the child.

The law as it stands is something of a hotchpotch. Only New South Wales, Victoria, South Australia and Western Australia have specific laws about reproductive technology. In the latter three states, centres that use reproductive technology to assist women to conceive must be licensed. Elsewhere, there may be no, or limited, licensing requirements and issues such as the parentage of children born as a result of assisted conception are incorporated as amendments in laws dealing with other matters. The NSW *Artificial Conception Act* was passed more than fifteen years ago in 1984 and so does not deal with many recent techniques and situations. Where a matter is not dealt with by statute, reproductive technology clinics mostly follow National Health and Medical Research Council (NHMRC) guidelines.

In-vitro fertilisation

In-vitro fertilisation (IVF), which literally means 'in glass', refers to ways in which conception is achieved outside the mother's body by the use of any suitable combination of donor semen and/or donor eggs. Sometimes, treatment with fertility drugs is appropriate for women who are infertile and may be used alone or combined with IVF.

The Australian Fertility Society has produced a code of conduct for IVF which is generally accepted.

Sometimes, both married couples and de facto couples will be accepted into an IVF program but in some states, such as Victoria, you must be legally married—although one clinic that implemented this rule was held to be in breach of the federal antidiscrimination legislation. There may be a definition of what constitutes a de facto couple—for example, in South Australia you must have been living together for at least five years to have access to reproductive technologies. The NHMRC guidelines say that procedures should be available to those in an 'accepted family relationship'.

Until recently, most clinics have defined 'couples' as heterosexual couples. However, in Queensland, a lesbian woman who had been refused access to an IVF program took action under the antidiscrimination legislation and was awarded $7500 compensation (the case is currently under appeal).

Victoria, South Australia and Western Australia prohibit the use of reproductive cells from a person who has died.

F and her husband, M, lived in Canberra. M was killed in a car accident while driving in Victoria. At the time of the accident, F was twenty-nine and M was thirty and they had no children although they had been married for several years. F decided she wanted the right to bear M's child. She did not want to make a decision to become pregnant at this time and might eventually decide against such a step but if the sperm were not removed from the body immediately, the option would not be available. She applied to the Victorian court for permission to harvest M's sperm. Permission was granted although according to Victorian law she could not use it to become impregnated. However, she could export it to New South Wales where there is no law forbidding her impregnation with the sperm—although since her husband is no longer alive to give his consent that may still arise as an issue.

Parentage and consent

In cases of in-vitro fertilisation or artificial insemination, the child is legally the child of the birth mother and her partner if he consents to the procedure. The consent of both parties is normally required before the procedure will be carried out. It is usually stated that the male donor is not the legal parent of the child. In Victoria, if the donor has a spouse, the spouse must also give written consent.

Records and information

Except in Victoria, South Australia and Western Australia, where there is a legal requirement for records of assisted conception to be kept, record-keeping is a matter for the clinic or the doctor. Some clinics maintain records, others destroy all records as a matter of policy. Generally the legislation provides that non-identifying information about the donor should be available to the couple and the child and, similarly, that non-identifying information about the child should be available to the donor. In Victoria, donors must provide identifying information that can later be accessed by their offspring. Everywhere, within these parameters, confidentiality is strictly preserved.

Surrogacy

Surrogacy occurs when a woman other than the natural mother carries a child who is usually conceived with either the eggs or sperm of the couple on whose behalf the baby is being carried. The child is then handed over to the mother at birth.

Particular issues arise in the case of surrogacy. Everywhere it is an offence to enter into a surrogacy arrangement for financial or other reward. It is also an offence to make arrangements for adoption without going through the official channels, so one woman can't bear a child on the basis that when the child is born another woman will adopt it. However, where the surrogacy arrangement is within the same family (e.g. between two sisters) an application to adopt a child may be viewed favourably, as it would be in any normal adoption.

Altruistic surrogacy arrangements where no fee or other reward is involved are sometimes allowed, depending on the state. The most frequent problem that arises is that the woman who carries the child changes her mind when the baby is born and refuses to give it up. In this case, the surrogacy agreement cannot usually be enforced and the birth mother cannot be forced to surrender the child. The Australian Capital Territory is the only jurisdiction so far to validate surrogacy contracts and make the genetic mother the legal mother, although other states, notably Western Australia, are considering similar legislation.

Mrs S offered to have a baby for her friend, Mrs Q, who had had a hysterectomy. Mrs S was impregnated with Mr Q's sperm. When the baby, E, was born in South Australia, Mr and Mrs Q were there and on her release from hospital took E to live with them in Brisbane. However, Mrs S underestimated how much giving up the baby would affect her and, seven months later, after grief counselling had not helped, she asked for E back. Mr and Mrs Q refused and the matter ended up in court, which found in favour of baby E's biological mother, Mrs S. The Q's were granted access. The judge said, 'It is apparent that this case is not about parenting capacity. The Court is dealing with four different personalities and quite different parenting styles. However, it is clear that each household has the capacity to provide a very high standard of care for E. Each of the adults loves the child and they are each committed to her welfare for the future. Simply stated, all of the parties wish to have the pleasure of raising this young girl'.

Formalities on birth

Registering a child's birth

You must register your child's birth with the Registry of Births, Deaths and Marriages. Depending on the state, the time limit for registration varies between one month and sixty days.

The child's name

In the case of married and de facto couples, it is more common than not for a child to have its father's surname. But the child can have its mother's surname if that is preferred. If the parents are not married, the father must agree to the child being given his surname.

Parents can choose the child's first names themselves. Occasionally, the registrar draws the line.

A couple who called themselves Rain and Moth wanted to call their daughter Crystal Lark. The registrar refused to let them register her birth because she did not have a surname. Rain and Moth contacted the ombudsman asking if the registrar could compel them to provide a surname. The ombudsman said that the registrar did have this right and they compromised by registering the birth with the surname Rain and making a declaration on the birth certificate that the child's full name was Crystal Lark.

Nationality

Your children who are born in Australia are Australian citizens if you are permanent residents here, even if your nationality is different. If you don't live permanently here, your children have the same nationality as you.

A child born overseas is an Australian, provided one of the parents was Australian at the time of the child's birth. However, the child's birth must be registered at an Australian consulate within five years. If you register the birth after this, you will have to complete extra formalities. If Australian citizenship isn't established by the time the child is eighteen, the child will have to apply for citizenship and comply with residency and other requirements in the same way as other applicants.

Paternity

The question of who is a child's father may be very important, especially when it comes to the question of who should support the child or whether the child has the right to inherit under a will.

If you are married, there is a legal presumption that your husband is the father of your children unless there is clear evidence that he could not have been the father—for example, he was overseas at the time of conception or there is a DNA or blood test showing he is not the father.

If you are unmarried, there must be a specific acknowledgment by the father of paternity. Many fathers wish to be named in the child's birth certificate. Alternatively, you can both complete a formal acknowledgment of fatherhood at any time before or after the baby is born. This can be done by a solicitor or at the community welfare department.

If the father won't acknowledge the child as his, you can apply to the court for a Declaration of Paternity. The court will require evidence. If you were living together at the time of conception that will usually be sufficient. If you were not living together but had an ongoing sexual relationship at the time of conception, that may be considered sufficient; however, if it was a casual affair you may have to establish that you were not sleeping with anyone else at the time.

Although R's name appeared on the birth certificate, when he and his partner J separated and she applied for child support, R was able to establish that he was not the father. R and J had met when J was eight months pregnant and R had agreed that the birth certificate should record his name as the father on the basis that they intended to marry and he would rear the child as his own. When they separated, R was able to satisfy the court that he had not met J at the time conception would have occurred.

Either party can ask for a blood or DNA test. The man can refuse the test, but the court is then entitled to infer that the reason for his refusal is that he thinks he might be the father. DNA tests are highly accurate and have virtually taken any element of guesswork out of paternity proceedings.

R had a brief affair with a married woman, L—they slept together twice—while L's husband was away. When she discovered she was pregnant L told her husband that he was not the father. Nevertheless, her husband was present when the baby was born and he later registered the birth showing himself as the father.

Some five years later, R made contact with L again, saying that he would like to resume their relationship and see the boy. When she rejected the proposals there was no further contact for some ten years when the relationship briefly resumed. At this time, L alleged that R asked on two occasions if he could take the boy on a trip around Australia and that she said she would only agree to this if her son were told that R was his real father, a suggestion that R rejected. R denied making the proposals but said that for the first time he was told he was the father of the boy.

When the boy was nearly eighteen, L, whose marriage had now ended, applied to the court for maintenance from R to enable her son to complete a university course. R tried to establish that he was not the father but went on to argue that, even if he was the biological father, it was unreasonable to require him to support at university an eighteen-year-old 'stranger'.

R refused to undergo blood and DNA tests. Taking his refusal into account and because intercourse had taken place at the relevant time, the judge was satisfied that R was the father of the boy. The judge went on to say that the fact that there had been no continuing relationship between the two did not mean that the boy was not entitled to be supported by his father while completing his education. The judge added that R could think himself fortunate that he had not been asked for support earlier.

Consent to adoption

Increasingly, the consent of an unmarried father is required if the child is to be adopted, although this depends on the state. Sometimes an unmarried father has a certain time in which to apply for custody of the child and, after that, he can't oppose the adoption. If the father's consent isn't required, he can apply to the court to stop the adoption. The court may take his wishes into account, but will make its decision according to the best interests of the child. Adoption orders are now sometimes made taking account of the natural father and giving him and the child the right to see one another. This is an area of the law that is changing rapidly and you will need to check with the adoption authorities.

Parenthood and your job

Barely a generation ago, once a woman became pregnant she was expected to resign from her job or she would almost certainly be sacked. Now discrimination on the grounds of pregnancy or parenthood is unlawful. If you want to continue working when you are pregnant or after you have the child, that is your choice. Nor can an employer insist that you move to a different job (e.g. out of the public eye) because you are pregnant.

Parental leave

In general, if you have worked for an employer for at least twelve months you are entitled to one year's unpaid maternity leave. It depends on the workplace but increasingly there is provision for up to fifty-two weeks' parental leave which can be taken by either parent, provided they have been in the job for at least twelve months. Both parents usually cannot take the leave together, except for the week of the child's birth.

A few firms are providing some paid maternity leave but this is a matter of human resources management policy and not a legal obligation.

In the case of either maternity leave or parental leave, when you return to work you are entitled to your old job back or, if that no longer exists, a job as close as possible in pay and status.

Flexible work practices

As an extension of the antidiscrimination laws, an employer may have to provide flexible work practices for employees responsible for young children, since not to do so may amount to indirect discrimination. If you are denied consideration because of family responsibilities, check with the antidiscrimination office.

chapter five

BRINGING UP CHILDREN

When you give birth to a child, you immediately take on responsibilities that last until the child turns eighteen and legally becomes an adult.

Doubtless there has always been a social expectation that parents will look after their children but until 1601 in Britain parents had no legal responsibility towards their offspring. In that year, the Poor Laws were passed, imposing a statutory obligation on parents to care for their children, but it must be said this had little to do with any concept of children's welfare; it simply enabled the poorhouses to recoup expenses from the parents of children who were sent there. The idea of children's rights was unheard of.

Now, of course, parents are more or less totally responsible for the welfare of their children and children's rights are an increasingly important part of the national legal and social fabric. There is sometimes an apparent conflict between what are regarded as parents' rights and children's rights.

In 1991 Australia signed the United Nations Convention on the Rights of the Child. This states that children should be brought up 'in the spirit of peace, dignity, tolerance, freedom, equality and solidarity'. The basic principles outlined in the Convention are:

- children have the right to life and to develop;
- children should have a say in decisions affecting them;
- children have the right to express their ideas and needs and to have their views taken seriously;
- children should not be treated less favourably than other members of the community just because they are young;
- all children have equal rights irrespective of race, colour, sex or religious beliefs;
- decisions about children must be in their best interests.

Some members of the community argue that the concept of children's rights has gone too far, that it impinges on parents' ability to discipline their children. Such people express outrage that it is now seemingly possible for children to 'divorce' their parents by asking the court for an order placing them in someone else's care. The outrage often overlooks the fact that such an order may be preferable to the child ending up on the streets, especially if living at home is impossible because of violence or sexual abuse. The relationship between parents and children is a particularly difficult one for the law to regulate. It isn't possible to legislate to make relationships work and there is often a fine line between ensuring that children are protected while, at the same time, ensuring that parents' right to rear their children in the way they choose is not unduly circumscribed.

Your rights and responsibilities

In broad terms, your rights regarding your children are:

- to raise and educate them in the way you think best;
- to impose reasonable discipline on them;

- to take legal action on their behalf;
- not to have them adopted by someone else without your consent.

Your responsibilities regarding your children are:

- to maintain them;
- to ensure that they get adequate medical care;
- to educate them.

Provided you follow these broad parameters, the law won't intervene in your dealings with your children unless you can't control them. If a child does not have a parent, a guardian will normally be appointed. In this case, the guardian has the same rights and responsibilities as if they were the child's parent.

Maintaining your children

Maintaining your children means providing adequate shelter, food and clothing, and appropriate medical care having regard to your resources.

If you don't maintain your children properly every effort will be made to help by providing counselling and social support but in the last resort it is an offence and you can be fined or imprisoned.

Schooling

You must normally send your children to school from the time they are six until they turn fifteen. If you decide on a state school, you may have to send them to a particular school, close to the area in which you live. Apart from this, you have the right to choose how your child will be educated and you may decide on a religious school or an independent school or a school such as a Montessori school that follows a particular educational philosophy.

Religion

You and your spouse have a joint right to decide on what religion, if any, your children will follow. By the age of about fourteen children can decide their religious affiliations for themselves. No court would order a teenager to follow their parents' religion against their wishes.

Discipline

You can discipline a child for misbehaviour, provided the punishment is reasonable. Keeping a child locked up for extended periods or inflicting excessive physical punishment is unreasonable and against the law. Anything other than a sharp slap on the hand or bottom with an open hand may be considered excessive. The law has been reluctant to make definite rules in this area of parent–child relationships, but corporal punishment is increasingly frowned on.

Children's earnings

Money earned by children is legally theirs. If your child has a regular job, you can insist that they contribute to board and lodging, according to how much they earn.

If you have a child earning a significant amount, for example, as a model or actor, generally a trustee is appointed. This is usually one or both parents. A trustee has an obligation to use the money for the benefit of the child. You may be able to use it for the child's maintenance—but it might be wise to get legal advice as the child can sue you once they turn eighteen if you use the money wrongly.

Contracts and leases

In general, young people under eighteen are not bound by contracts or leases unless it is for their benefit. In practice, a young person renting a flat can probably sign a binding lease but usually the landlord will want a guarantee from a parent. Similarly, people doing business with under-eighteen-year-olds will usually require a guarantor, such as a parent. This means that you will be liable if your child defaults on the lease or contract.

Alcohol

Young people under eighteen are not allowed on licensed premises, and nor are they permitted to collect or buy liquor. So you risk a fine if you send your teenager to pick up the grog from the bottle shop.

Leaving home

In theory, your authority over your children lasts until they turn eighteen. In practice, once they are fifteen or sixteen it is difficult to stop them leaving home. Welfare authorities may intervene if a young person under eighteen is in danger or asks for help but they won't usually force them to return home against their wishes.

In a few instances, a young person has successfully applied to the court for an order saying that the relationship with their parents has irretrievably broken down, and someone else has been appointed as their guardian. This is a controversial law, with many people objecting to the fact that children can effectively 'divorce' their parents. But the court won't make an order without very good reasons—certainly not simply that the child is temporarily out of sorts with the parents. It may be a better option than the child living on the streets.

Medical care

If your child is ill you have a duty to get necessary medical care.

Your consent is normally necessary before medical treatment can be carried out on your child but, if you withhold consent and the doctor considers that the child's life is in danger, the doctor can go ahead and perform the treatment anyway. A religious belief against certain forms of treatment (e.g. against blood transfusions) is not a ground on which you can deny the child treatment. If necessary, a court order can be obtained enabling the treatment to take place.

Can your daughter have an abortion without you knowing?

The answer to this is probably *yes*. Although, strictly speaking, young people do not become adults until they turn eighteen, in the case of medical treatment they can consent on their own behalf if they are mature enough to understand the nature and consequences of the treatment. A girl of fourteen or fifteen will normally be considered to have the necessary maturity, although it depends on the girl and the doctor's assessment of the situation. In New South Wales, young people over fourteen have a legal right to consent to their own general medical treatment.

Even if a teenager can't find a private doctor to carry out the abortion, she can probably have the procedure done at a family planning clinic.

Doctors are bound by the same rules of confidentiality in relation to young patients as adult patients. If a doctor were to tell you without your daughter's consent that she was planning or had had an abortion, the doctor would be in breach of an ethical rule and subject to disciplinary action.

Contraceptives

It is generally accepted that a doctor can prescribe contraceptives for a girl over the age of about fourteen without informing her parents. Condoms can be bought over the counter at a chemist or from a vending machine without parental involvement or an age check (see also Chapter Ten, *Sex*).

Child abuse

If you or your spouse physically abuse your child you can be charged with an offence and, in extreme cases, the child will be removed from your care. Professionals, such as doctors, teachers and social workers, may be required to report suspected cases of child abuse. Child abuse includes having sex with a child.

While welfare authorities try to solve these problems without recourse to the law, if all efforts fail there may be no alternative but to ask the court for an order placing the child in the care of the state.

Increasingly, abusive parents are the subject of legal action, often when the victim has reached adulthood and years after they have left home.

Children in need of care

Children who are not properly cared for by their parents can be placed in the care of the state, which usually means they will be sent to live with a relative or in a foster home or government institution. Applications for children to be taken into care are sometimes made by parents. Whether the application is made by the welfare authorities or the parents, the best interests of the child is the primary factor the court considers when making a decision. Whenever possible, the court will take into account the child's wishes, the importance of maintaining contact with the parents and preserving the child's cultural environment.

Children in trouble

It can be devastating for parents to find that their child is in trouble with the law. Sometimes this may be for relatively minor misdemeanours, sometimes the charges are more serious. Whatever the charge, young people under eighteen are normally treated differently by the law on the basis that they are not as responsible for their actions as are adults. The laws in different states vary but the broad principles are the same.

Often the first inkling parents have that their child is in trouble is when the police arrive at the door. If this happens to you, you should be polite and courteous and aware of your child's rights. You do not have to answer questions, especially if you think it may incriminate your child. However, you will probably want to cooperate as far as you can. Apart from the fact that the police have a difficult job to do, they are more likely to treat the matter sympathetically if they can see that a child has a supportive family who are not being obstructive.

In the same way as adults, young people who are stopped by the police do not have to answer questions unless they are driving a motor vehicle, in which case they must give police their name and address, produce their licence and give details of the accident or other incident. This does not mean they have to admit they were in the wrong but they should politely tell the police what happened.

Similarly, if a child is arrested they do not have to answer questions. They should say politely that they would prefer not to say anything until a lawyer is present. If a young person under eighteen makes a confession or statement, it is not admissible as evidence unless an adult of the child's choosing or a lawyer is present.

Often young people are let off with a caution. If a caution is not appropriate and the police decide to press ahead with the charge, young people will normally be allowed home on bail, except in very serious cases.

Except in very serious cases, young people are dealt with in a special children's court. All children are entitled to free legal advice from the duty solicitor who will be at the court on the morning of the hearing.

If the child is found guilty of an offence, a punishment will be imposed. Traditionally, children's courts have taken a more lenient approach to punishment and the likelihood is, unless the young person has offended many times before, they will receive a bond. In some cases, the young person will be required to do unpaid work for the community, usually with a charity or community organisation. Prison for young people is regarded as a last resort and every emphasis is placed on rehabilitation.

Disputes about children

In any case where the court is asked to rule on a dispute between parents in relation to a child, the court will decide according to the best interests of the child. This is particularly the case in family law matters where the child's interests, not the parents' interests, are the overriding consideration.

Inheritance rights

In relation to inheritance there is no distinction between a child born to married parents and a child born to unmarried parents. If an ex-nuptial child is not adequately provided for in a parent's will, the child can claim on the estate in the same way as a nuptial child. The only difference in relation to a child born to unmarried parents is that the child may sometimes have to prove that they are the child of their father. Of course, if the father is named on the birth certificate or has otherwise acknowledged the child, there is no problem.

Right to take legal action

Children under eighteen can't take legal action in their own name. This doesn't mean that they have no right to sue, but simply that the action must be taken on their behalf by an adult, usually a parent.

Although it rarely happens, children can make their own applications to the Family Court regarding who they should live with, their right to see a parent and all the other matters the court deals with when parents separate. Children are often provided with their own lawyer who represents their interests in the Family Court.

Children can sue their parents if they are injured because of the parent's negligence—for example, in a car accident. In one case, an eighteen-year-old girl sued her mother for an accident that happened before she was born.

> Janine S was five months pregnant with her daughter Kylie when she was driving a utility as part of a cattle muster on the family

property. She lost control of the vehicle and it careered down a slope colliding with a bank. She lost consciousness and only regained it in hospital. Shortly after Kylie was born four months later she was diagnosed with cerebral palsy. Through her grandmother, Kylie sued her mother for damages.

The judge was satisfied that the accident was caused by Janine's carelessness and that Kylie's cerebral palsy was due to the accident. He then had to decide if Kylie could be awarded compensation since she was not born at the time. He decided that it should not make any difference. Kylie would have been entitled to compensation if the accident had happened four months after she was born; there seemed no good reason why she should not have the same right four months before she was born. Kylie was awarded $2.8 million dollars in compensation.

For the most part, actions by children against their parents have been limited to cases where the parent is insured. Traditionally, there has been opposition to a general right of action by children against parents because of the socially negative consequences likely to flow from such actions. However, as community attitudes evolve, this may change.

Other actions involving unborn children have been taken against doctors. In one New South Wales case, the child had not even been conceived. In the case, the mother was suffering from syphilis and when she became pregnant her child contracted the disease from her and was born severely deformed. The gynaecologist was held to be negligent because he had not had the necessary tests performed on the mother.

part three

When love flies out the window

chapter six

ENDING A MARRIAGE

When we marry, most of us think it will be for life. The reality is that more than one-third of first marriages will end in divorce.

There are three ways a marriage comes to an end: you agree to separate, you leave your spouse, your spouse leaves you. Whichever, it is likely to be a period of sadness, loneliness, emotional stress and often financial difficulty. Since the *Family Law Act* was passed in 1975, the legal process of divorce is easier than it used to be, but the emotional pain is still there and in the middle of all the tension there are countless things you have to think about and organise. You will need to consider where each spouse will live, how you will live, who pays the mortgage and all the other financial matters that will probably have been intertwined while you were together. If you have children you will have their needs and welfare to consider as well.

By far the best way to solve matters on separation is to talk about everything calmly and find solutions that are mutually acceptable. Most couples can do this and ninety-five per cent of Australian divorces are settled amicably without having to be contested in court. Even if the separation is amicable, if you know what the legal position is you can both do what has to be done in a way that ensures that neither of you sacrifices your legal rights.

The courts will not deal with any of the matters relating to the breakdown of a marriage in a spirit of 'punishment'. For the most part, it is irrelevant whether you or your spouse has been a 'good' or 'bad' spouse, or whether you have had an affair or are involved in a new relationship. Especially if your spouse has left you for someone else, you may be feeling angry and hurt and consider they should 'pay' for their behaviour. However, the court will not make moral judgments and will want to establish only that your marriage has broken down, not the reasons behind the breakdown. In considering financial matters the court will base its decisions on what you need and what your spouse can afford; in considering arrangements for the children the court will decide according to what is best for them.

What do we have to do to separate?

All you have to do to separate is start living apart. It is as simple as that. There are no formal steps involved and no formal documentation. However, it should be made clear that the marriage is at an end. This is no big deal if you both agree but, if one of you is leaving against the wishes of the other, then the spouse who is leaving should tell the other spouse that they consider the marriage is over—preferably in a written note so that there is a record. When the time comes for a divorce, the court will want to be satisfied that the marriage has broken down irretrievably and that you have been separated for the required period of twelve months. Unless there is some written evidence, it is open to a spouse who doesn't want a divorce to argue that the marriage isn't really over, you simply left in a huff or some such thing, and to dispute when separation occurred. In that case, you may have to start the period of separation again.

Even if you are ending your marriage by mutual consent, keep a note of the date you separate. The court will want to know, and you may have forgotten in a year's time when you apply for a divorce.

There is no longer any such thing as a 'legal separation' in the sense of a sort of halfway house between marriage and divorce. Before the *Family Law Act* was passed, this was mostly used by people who wanted some acknowledgment that their marriage was over but who had religious objections to divorce. It enabled property and such matters to be dealt with, which at that time could only be dealt with on divorce. Now property and other matters can be dealt with at any time and a couple who wish to separate but don't want to proceed to divorce, for whatever reason, simply start living apart and make whatever arrangements as to money and children they think appropriate in the same way as any other couple whose marriage has ended.

Who should leave?

If possible, you should agree on who leaves. If the decision to separate is taken by one spouse this may be difficult—but the fact that one spouse initiates the separation doesn't mean they have to be the one to leave. From the point of view of rights and responsibilities *vis-à-vis* money and children, the question of who leaves whom doesn't matter although it may have practical ramifications.

What about the family home?

Each spouse has the right to a fair share of any assets acquired during the marriage, including the home, and the fact that one spouse moves out doesn't affect these rights. Even if the home is in only one name, that doesn't give that spouse the right to turn the other spouse out, and nor does it give that spouse any greater rights to the home in the long term. From a practical point of view, however, there may be advantages in being the spouse who stays, if only because life is probably difficult enough without having to find and settle into somewhere new. Make sure you have adequate arrangements in place for the mortgage to be paid. If the payments get behind, the bank or finance company can force you to sell up.

Can one spouse force the other spouse to leave?

Your spouse may agree to move out, even if you are the one ending the marriage, but it is difficult for one spouse to force the other spouse out of the home. You need a court order and courts do not like saying that a person cannot live in their own home, unless there are very good reasons. A good reason might be if your spouse was being violent, in which case you may be granted a sole occupation order.

What about the furniture?

In general, the court considers that you are each entitled to half the furniture. If you move out, you will need some furniture to get established in your new home and it is preferable if you and your spouse can agree on what you should take. If you can't agree on individual items, one way of solving the impasse is to compile two fairly equal lists and draw them out of a hat. If agreement or even discussion is impossible, you may have no choice but to act unilaterally and take what is your due. If either spouse gets more than the other, this will usually be adjusted in the property settlement.

What about support?

If you have no means of support on separation, you can apply to the court for an urgent maintenance order. This will normally be granted if you have children under five to care for, are incapacitated, ill or too old to get a job (but see below for a fuller explanation of maintenance).

If you need support for your children you should apply to the Child Support Agency. If you need money urgently, you can apply to the Family Court but you must have applied to the Child Support Agency first.

Violence

If you are subjected to violence you can get a court order forbidding your spouse to live in the home or approach you at home or at work. Orders are available from the Family Court but it is usually quicker and easier to get an order from the local magistrates' court.

Separating under the same roof

You can separate while you are both living under the same roof, provided the relationship of marriage no longer exists. Basically, this means that you don't sleep together or socialise together and generally that you don't behave as a married couple behaves. Sleeping in separate bedrooms might be an important indication that the marriage is over but it is not necessarily enough by itself. The court will look at the whole picture including whether you still behave like a married couple—for example, by giving one another help and support, how you present in public, whether you continue to share the household tasks, if you have joint financial responsibilities and so on.

Similarly, the fact that you sleep together occasionally may not be important if it is clear the marriage is over, and nor will it be important if you share some of the chores from time to time. The crucial thing is the marriage relationship in all its aspects.

When a divorce application is heard under these circumstances, the court may want corroboration that the marriage is over, perhaps from a friend or relative—but *not* the children if they are under eighteen. A sworn statement may be enough corroboration, but sometimes the court will want the witness to be there.

Generally, the court will believe what the spouse applying for the divorce says unless it has reason not to. If one spouse says you are separated and the other spouse says you are not, then the court will want evidence to establish the truth.

If you intend staying under the same roof while you are separated, you should see a lawyer to find out what steps to take.

Trying again

After you separate you can have one try at making your marriage work without having to start the separation period again. However, the period you are together won't be counted as part of the separation. For example, if you separate for six months, resume living together for a month, and then decide that the marriage really is over, you must be separated for another six months before you can apply for the divorce. You can only resume living together for one period without having to start the separation period again, unless it is for a very short period of time, when the court might decide it shouldn't count.

What about the children?

Both parents are jointly responsible for the children unless the court orders otherwise. Generally, the children will fare better if you can agree on who they will live with and where. It is also better if you can agree about their support—but, if not, the parent who has the children should apply immediately to the Child Support Agency for an assessment as to how much the other parent should pay (see Chapter Eight, *When parents separate*).

Joint bank accounts

As a general rule, you are each entitled to half the money in a joint bank account. However, unless you have an arrangement with the bank in which the signature of both spouses is necessary for transactions, it is vital to remember that either spouse can draw out all the money without the permission of the other. It is best to agree on how the money is to be divided and then to close the account. Even if you and your spouse are on good terms, the relationship may deteriorate—settle it early on.

If your spouse does take more than their share of the joint account, it will be taken into account in the property settlement, so you won't necessarily lose in the long term—but it is quicker, cheaper and easier not to put it to the test.

Joint debts

You are each wholly responsible for any debts held in joint names—note, you are each responsible for the whole debt, not just half of it. So if your spouse defaults on the debt, you can be required by the lender to pay the lot. Again, this will be taken into account in the property settlement but in the meantime you may be saddled with repayments you can ill afford. Try to work out a mutually acceptable way that debts are to be paid. Close any joint credit accounts as soon as you separate.

Requirements for a divorce

The only requirement for a divorce is that your marriage has broken down irretrievably with no prospect of reconciliation. The way you establish this is by living apart for twelve months. Nothing else is necessary. The court is not interested in why the marriage broke down, whose fault it was, who left whom, whether either of you behaved badly or had an affair.

Marriages of less than two years

If you have been married for less than two years before you apply for a divorce, you may be required to have marriage counselling, unless you can persuade the court that there are special circumstances in your case—for example, that your spouse has been violent towards you. The main things the court will consider in deciding whether you should have counselling are whether you have genuinely tried to make the marriage work and whether counselling will help save the marriage. Note that the two-year period relates to when you file the application—and you must be separated for at least one year before you can do this. So, in effect, counselling is only compulsory if you have been married for less than one year before you separate.

Opposing a divorce

There are only limited grounds on which you can oppose a divorce:

- that you have not been separated for at least twelve months;
- that reconciliation is possible;
- that the arrangements for the children are not proper.

None of these reasons will stop the divorce forever, they will only delay it. If your spouse alleges that you have not been separated for twelve months, you will either have to prove them wrong by producing evidence of when separation occurred, or you will have to start the period of separation again. Even if you are forced to take the latter course of action, at the most you will only have to wait for another twelve months before the divorce can go through.

Almost by definition, reconciliation depends on both parties being willing to try. If you say that reconciliation is possible but your spouse says it isn't, the court will normally accept that reconciliation is not possible. In some circumstances, the court may order that you both attend counselling, but if you then say that the marriage is at an end the divorce will normally go ahead even if the other spouse continues to oppose it.

The court will want to be satisfied that the arrangements for the children are proper before it will grant a divorce, but the court won't necessarily decide the arrangements are not proper just because one spouse opposes them. The court will only consider the arrangements are not proper if the children are not being adequately cared for. If there is an argument over the arrangements for the children, the court will normally grant the divorce and then hear the dispute about the children at a later date.

When can an application for divorce be made?

You can apply for a divorce the day after the twelve-month period of separation is up. For example, if you separate on

1 January in one year, you can apply for a divorce on 2 January the following year (or the next working day).

Who should apply?

Either spouse can apply for a divorce or you can make a joint application. The applicant pays the costs involved so it may make sense for the spouse who can afford it best to make the application. If you make a joint application you can agree to share the costs or the spouse with more money may think it fair to meet the entire cost even though you are applying for the divorce together.

As part of the application you must give details of your marriage, your separation and any children of the marriage. You will also have to say whether there are any other legal proceedings currently taking place between you and your spouse—for example, in relation to domestic violence or child welfare.

If only one spouse applies for the divorce, the documents must be served on the other spouse so that they know what is happening and have a chance to object to the application. The documents can be posted (by registered mail to avoid your spouse denying that they have been received), or delivered by a friend or relative or professional process server. You may not serve the documents personally. The spouse receiving the documents must be given at least twenty-eight days' notice of the date the divorce is to be heard, or forty-two days' notice if they are overseas.

Once the documents have been received, the other spouse must respond in a particular way, set out in the forms.

If you can't find your spouse

If you don't know where your spouse is, you must take reasonable steps to find them. For example, you should contact their family, friends or employer. You can have a search made of motor vehicle registration and licence records. If you can't find your spouse despite making reasonable efforts you can ask the court to grant the divorce even though the documents have not been served.

What is the cost?

The Family Court filing fees are currently about $550. If you can't afford this, you can apply for the fee to be waived. As well you may have to pay for having the documents served on your spouse, together with the cost of obtaining the necessary supporting documents such as your marriage certificate.

If you engage a solicitor, it will probably cost between $2000 and $4000 for an uncomplicated divorce, including agreements about children and money. If you have only one or two consultations just to ensure that you are being treated fairly and that the documents are in order you may be charged less than this. If you end up fighting through the courts over property or children, the costs may add up to many thousands of dollars.

Because, in theory at least, there are no winners and losers in divorce it is rare for one spouse to be ordered to pay the other spouse's legal fees. They will, however, be taken into account in the property settlement. If one spouse is unreasonable in their attitude to the children and property, so that court proceedings are unnecessarily prolonged, they may be ordered to pay the other spouse's legal costs.

In some circumstances, your lawyer may have to provide a costs estimate at the beginning or ongoing costs estimates as the case proceeds. The court has been reviewing previous rules in this regard and you should ask your lawyer what the current position is.

It will help to keep your costs down if you are well prepared for your consultations. Make sure you have a list of your assets and liabilities and those of your spouse. You should know the date you separated and be able to give a clear statement of what arrangements have been made for the children. Be aware that your lawyer is there to tell you what your legal rights and obligations are and what choices of action you may have. Of course, it may be relevant to tell your lawyer the facts of the break-up and hopefully she will be sympathetic and understanding but remember that most lawyers charge according to time and they are not trained counsellors. Furthermore moral outrage is unlikely to have any legal relevance. If you want to spend hours unburdening yourself about your spouse's shortcomings, it will cost you money and you are better off consulting a counsellor—or talking to a friend.

Need for a lawyer

If your divorce is simple and straightforward, without any dispute over children or money matters, you can arrange it yourself. About one-third of divorces are dealt with in this way.

Even if you agree on what should happen and intend to appear for yourself in court, getting a lawyer to check out the proposed arrangements may be sensible. Sometimes one partner agrees to less than they are entitled to, either to avoid being seen as aggressive or because they don't know what their rights are.

If you are making a child support agreement, especially if it involves assets, you should consult a lawyer to avoid later difficulties.

If you can't agree about arrangements for the children or what is a fair financial settlement or if you are still living under the same roof, then you will need to see a lawyer.

Getting a divorce the DIY way

Divorce kits are available from the Family Court. There is one kit for couples with children under eighteen and another kit for couples whose children are over eighteen.

The forms are a mixture of fill-in-the-blanks and tick-the-boxes.

The form for children under eighteen asks you for details of the children, where they live and your arrangements for their housing, supervision, the contact with each parent, their financial support, education and health care. Staff may help with filling in the forms correctly but they can't give legal advice.

You will need certified copies of your marriage and birth certificates. If you were born overseas you may need an Australian citizenship certificate. If you were married overseas you will need the documents relating to your marriage; if necessary the documents will have to be translated.

Once the forms are filled out you have to affirm or swear the application in front of a JP, a solicitor or anyone authorised to witness affidavits. You then file three copies with the Family Court together with a copy of your marriage certificate and the filing fee.

If you haven't made a joint application, once the documents are filed you will have to arrange for them to be served on your spouse and swear an affidavit that this has been done. The kits explain how. Then you wait for the hearing, usually three or more months away. Provided there are no complicating factors, you will normally be granted the divorce at the hearing.

The Family Court

Divorce and all the ancillary matters are heard in the Family Court, a specialist court established by the *Family Law Act* (see Chapter Fourteen, *The courts*).

Family Court proceedings

When you file the application with the court, you will be given a return date—which is the date the case will come before the court. This will be at least several weeks away. If your case is straightforward it will normally be heard and a decision reached on this day. If you say your marriage has broken down, the court will normally believe you unless there is good reason not to. The court will only want to be satisfied that you have been separated for the required twelve months and that the necessary formalities have been complied with.

If your spouse opposes the divorce, or the documents are not in order, or your spouse has not received the necessary notice the case will be put off (adjourned) to a later date, usually some weeks or months away. If you have children under eighteen years of age, the court will want to be satisfied about the arrangements for their care before it will grant the divorce. This doesn't mean that the court will want to override the arrangements you have already made; unless these are grossly inadequate the court won't substitute its judgment for yours.

You can get a divorce even if you haven't resolved property issues and finally decided on the arrangements for the children. These can be heard at a later date.

If you have a solicitor acting for you, the solicitor will take care of all the documentation and appear in court on your behalf (although, depending on the circumstances, you may need to be there). If you don't have a solicitor, you will have to do it all yourself. If you are simply seeking an uncomplicated divorce, you can probably do it yourself quite easily. If you are arguing over property or the children, you will normally need a lawyer to put your case. In disputed cases, the delay may be many months or even years.

Although divorce is psychologically a major event for most people in that it is the step that finally ends a relationship that was entered into with such high hopes, in a legal sense divorce is simply the formal recognition that the marriage is over. It may take only a few minutes.

You may not even have to attend the court if your spouse has applied for the divorce. In theory, neither spouse has to attend if there are no children under eighteen but in practice at least one spouse should be there to answer any questions the court has. If there are questions and no one is there to answer them, the matter will be adjourned and the divorce will be delayed. Despite the need for this precaution, if the documents have been correctly filled in the court will usually have all the information it needs and in most cases will grant the divorce without further ado.

When does the divorce become final?

A divorce is granted in two stages. The first stage is when the court grants what is called a decree nisi. This means that the divorce is granted but it doesn't become final for one month, when a decree absolute is issued. The decree absolute is usually a formality and a copy will be sent either to the applicant or their solicitor. The respondent can also request a copy. It is possible to appeal before the decree absolute is issued but there are very limited grounds on which this can be done. You can't remarry until the decree absolute is issued.

Counselling and mediation

The philosophy underpinning the Family Court is that people should be helped to resolve their own problems on divorce and that having the court decide on what should happen should be the last resort. Courts are expensive and emotionally taxing. Decisions imposed by a court inevitably imply a 'winner' and a 'loser' and at least one party will almost always be dissatisfied. The Family Court offers conciliation counselling and mediation as a way of avoiding court involvement.

Counselling is usually used in relation to children and is a way of solving disputes with the help of a counsellor trained in relationship therapy. You may decide to try counselling yourself or the court may order it. Counselling sessions are confidential and lawyers may not usually attend.

Mediation is used in disputes over property, maintenance or children. It is cheaper and quicker than court action. For it to be successful you should both be committed to working out your differences in this way and be reasonably equal in terms of bargaining strength and ability. Mediators don't suggest or impose solutions but find ways to make work the solutions you agree on. You are in charge of the outcome, the mediator's task is to control the process. Mediation won't work unless both parties can put their position clearly or if one party is likely to be overborne by the other. You can refuse to accept a solution put forward by your partner if you think it is unfair, and you can abandon the entire process at any time.

There may be up to three mediation sessions. The mediating team usually consists of one lawyer and one social worker or psychologist, one of whom will be male and the other female. You may have your lawyer at the mediation sessions but you don't have to. At present, mediation isn't available in all courts.

To apply for Family Court counselling or mediation, you simply fill in a form available from the Court. If the matter involves children, you may be able to make an appointment by phone. Waiting times are sometimes several weeks.

Counselling services are also provided by independent organisations including Relationships Australia and Centacare. Some lawyers also act as mediators. The Family Court has a list of approved counselling and mediation services.

Money matters

When your marriage breaks down, money matters inevitably have to be dealt with. The fact that love has flown out the window doesn't mean that you can't be civil but discussions over money are often the point at which civility disappears. Divorce is not only an emotional kick in the teeth, it is almost always a financial jolt as well. The average length of marriages that end in divorce is eleven years. The chances are you will have just started to feel financially secure. Now you face the prospect of losing a substantial proportion of the assets you have built up. It may help to avoid the aggro if you know what the law requires you to do.

Assets acquired during the marriage must be divided as fairly as possible, and if one spouse has been the breadwinner with the other spouse out of the workforce, the question of maintenance will arise. Support must be provided for any children.

In theory, money matters are divided into property (division of the assets) and maintenance (ongoing support). In practice, the distinction is often blurred and, for example, a property settlement may take into account the need of one spouse for maintenance and so give that spouse a larger share of the assets to enable an income to be provided.

As with all matters related to divorce, it is best if you can agree between yourselves as to what is fair. If you can agree you can have a formal written agreement drawn up and either registered with the court so that it can be enforced or made the subject of a consent order by the court. The documents should be drawn up by a lawyer to ensure they reflect what you want them to say and that your basic rights are protected. If you can't agree, and fight it out in court, you may end up spending most of the available money on lawyers' fees. Also the court doesn't know your circumstances nearly as well as you do. Of course, you will each be given the opportunity to state your case but there is no way a court can fully appreciate the subtleties of your situation in a few hours.

When can we deal with money matters?

You can deal with money matters as soon as you have agreed on what should happen; you don't have to wait for the divorce.

However, it can't be left for too long after the divorce. An application for a maintenance or property order must be made within twelve months of the divorce. Once the twelve months have elapsed the court will only allow an application if there is a satisfactory explanation of why it was not made before, and if there are special circumstances—for example, hardship would result if the application were not allowed.

What principles apply to property settlements?

The principle underlying all property settlements is that each spouse is entitled to a fair share of any property acquired during the marriage. It does not matter whose name the property is in or who paid for it: each spouse is entitled to a fair share.

There is no predetermined formula in Australia as there is in some countries (e.g. a 50/50 split) since it is considered preferable to sacrifice some certainty in the interests of ensuring that individual circumstances can be taken into account. Usually the parent who has the children is entitled to more than 50 per cent of the assets since they have the greater expense and will almost certainly have their earning capacity affected by the responsibilities of childrearing.

As a general rule, any property you acquired during the marriage is regarded as belonging to both of you. This applies particularly to the family home; it doesn't matter whose name the home is in, you are both considered to be owners. In theory, property you each owned before the marriage remains yours individually but as time passes individual ownership becomes less important. In marriages that have lasted a long time most, if not all, property will be considered as jointly owned. In the case of heirlooms or similar items, you can probably establish a claim for them to remain in your possession, but the value will be taken into account in the property settlement so you may have to sacrifice something else. If the only way a fair property settlement can be achieved is to sell property that one of you owns personally, this is what may have to happen.

What property do we divide?

All property should be taken into account. This includes any real estate, including the family home, shares and other investments, jewellery, cars, furniture, superannuation and life assurance policies. If you think your spouse might try to hide assets to avoid them being counted, tell your lawyer. There are ways to find out the true position but you will need legal advice. If your home or other assets are in the name of your spouse, there may be a danger your spouse will try to sell that asset to prevent you from getting your share. If you suspect that this may happen, *see a lawyer without delay*. It can be stopped but it is essential to act quickly—once the sale has been completed it may be difficult to do much.

Superannuation

Don't overlook superannuation. If you or your spouse has future super entitlements, which you would have shared if you had remained together, this should be built in to the property settlement. Super isn't easy to deal with. A typical situation is that one partner has, say, $400 000 invested in a super fund which cannot be accessed until retirement. The other assets are a home and savings of roughly the same amount. Generally, the non-superannuated partner gets to keep the home and savings and the superannuated partner gets the super. The result is that one partner is left with no cash and the other partner has no retirement savings. Proposed legislation is aimed at dealing with the matter in a fairer way but finding a satisfactory mechanism for doing this is proving hard. In the meantime, the courts have made it clear that super is not to be ignored.

S and C had been married for nearly twenty-five years and were aged 54 and 69 when they decided to separate. The two children of the marriage were in their twenties and living independent lives. The assets were considerable—worth over $6 million, including a family home valued at more than $1.5 million. The husband, C, had operated a restaurant owned by a family company which employed both him and his wife and operated a superannuation scheme on their behalf. There were also long service leave entitlements.

When the court was asked to decide on a property settlement, it was decided that S was entitled to 50 per cent of the matrimonial home and 30 per cent of the remaining property. This would yield about $1.6 million for her and about $2.8 million for C. As far as the superannuation/long service leave was concerned, they were each entitled to the respective payouts they would receive in the normal course of events with no adjustment for the divorce.

S appealed. She did not dispute the property settlement in other respects, but she said the superannuation should have been treated in the same way as the other assets. The trial judge's assessment of the property division other than the home was based on the contribution of the parties over the years and this had led to the 70/30 per cent apportionment. S argued that this apportionment should also apply to the superannuation. The Full Court hearing the appeal agreed and awarded her another $115 000.

Prospective inheritances

The question of what to do if your spouse is expected to inherit substantial assets isn't quite so easy to resolve. Where the inheritance is likely to occur in the reasonably near future, the court may defer a decision until it happens. If the inheritance is expected to be many years down the track, deferring the decision is probably impractical. There is also the question of finding out what the inheritance is likely to be. The fact that great-uncle Fred says that he intends to leave you all his worldly goods is not much of a guide to the court if it doesn't know how much his worldly goods are worth. The courts are reluctant to force people who are not otherwise involved in the case to produce their financial records. And, of course, great-uncle Fred might change his mind before he dies and leave his worldly goods to somebody else. Generally the court will try to make a fair allocation taking the circumstances into account, as far as they can be ascertained.

How do we decide what is fair?

The best way to decide what is fair is to apply the same principles as the court would apply. Broadly, these can be summed up as:

- the contribution each of you has made to the marriage; and
- your respective income needs both now and in the future.

Contribution does not mean only financial contribution but includes looking after the home and family. The law clearly states that a spouse who stays at home to care for the family makes just as much contribution to the acquisition of assets as the spouse who goes out to work and earns the money to pay for them.

A major factor in deciding income needs is who the children live with. Clearly, if you have the children you need more income to look after them and you probably have fewer opportunities to develop a career and earn a high income. Consequently, you are likely to be entitled to a larger proportion of the assets. A parent with young children will not usually be expected to work, but a parent of schoolage children may be.

Other factors that are relevant in assessing income needs are the age and health of you and your spouse. If you are old and ill you may not be able to work and you may have greater income needs than a spouse who is relatively young and fit.

The fact that a spouse has been out of the workforce may be a relevant factor. However, this is not always given as much weight as it used to be. In general, a spouse who is fit enough is expected to get a job, even if they haven't worked for many years, and at least contribute to their own support.

Behaviour is only an issue in property division if it has affected either spouse's contribution to the marriage. For example, if you have gambled away the family assets it might affect the amount of property you are reasonably entitled to on divorce, especially if your spouse has been a prudent and careful money manager. However, the fact that you or your spouse has had an affair or is involved in a new relationship is unlikely of itself to be a relevant factor.

The court has recently held that if a spouse takes a lower-paying job after separation, perhaps with the deliberate intention of paying less spouse maintenance or child support, it is appropriate for that spouse to pay an amount based on what they are capable of earning. While future decisions will depend on the facts of any given case, in that instance, the judge said that 'if a man is prepared to work eighty hours a week while his family is together, there is no basis on which the court can say that he should be excused from that productivity when the marriage breaks down'.

A family business or farm

A family business or farm will be dealt with in the same way as other property. It is often best if one spouse can buy out the other spouse but, if this is not possible, the business may have to be sold and the proceeds divided. Until recently, courts were often reluctant to force the sale of a business or farm which may have been in the family for generations. Now the court will take this into account—but if the only way to ensure that the assets can be divided fairly is to sell the business or farm, this is what the court will order.

Finality of property orders

In general, once a property order is made, it is final. You can't go back to the court later and say it was unfair, so make sure you understand fully what is happening. There are some circumstances when an order can be changed—for example, if one spouse did not disclose significant assets—but this is rare.

Stamp duty

When property is transferred between spouses as a result of divorce, it is exempt from the usual stamp duty provisions. However, there must be a Family Court order for this to apply. If you have finalised your property settlement before the divorce and have already paid stamp duty, you can claim a refund when the divorce actually takes place.

Enforcing a property order

If your spouse does not comply with a property order, it can be enforced. If necessary, the property can be transferred to you without your spouse's signature, or it can be seized and sold. Ask your lawyer for advice.

Spouse maintenance

Maintenance is an amount of money paid by one spouse to the other for support. When you separate you are not automatically entitled to maintenance and, indeed, if you are not caring for young children and are able to work, you may be expected to support yourself. You may sometimes be entitled to maintenance for a specified period of time—for example, to acquire some workplace skills or to retrain.

Maintenance for you and support for the children are two different matters. Both spouses are expected to support the children and the amount the non-resident parent is expected to pay is calculated by the Child Support Agency according to a formula, unless you agree on something different.

Lump sum maintenance

If possible, maintenance will be awarded as a lump sum which can be invested to earn interest and provide an income. This means that you no longer need to have any dealings with one another and can get on with your lives. It also has the advantage that it doesn't disappear if your spouse dies, disappears or becomes unemployed. It has the disadvantage that if you become ill or lose your job, it can't be increased. On the other hand, nor can your spouse demand it back if you inherit a fortune from long-lost Uncle Harry.

Periodic maintenance

Of course, the court can't order a lump sum if there aren't any assets or money to pay it. In this case, it is possible that periodic payments will be awarded—but only if you really need it and your spouse can afford it. If you will be getting periodic maintenance make sure that cost of living increases are built in to the order. It is possible for periodic maintenance to be changed, but only if circumstances change significantly—for example, the spouse paying it becomes unemployed. In rare circumstances it may be increased—for example, if you get sick and can't work any more—but you will have to establish that your former spouse can afford the increase. It is unlikely that maintenance will be increased just because your former spouse gets a salary increase—you will have to show that you really need the extra money.

Maintenance and social security

Before you can get social security you have to show that you have tried to get maintenance from your spouse. The taxpayer is not expected to support you if your spouse can afford to. You also have to comply with any other regulations. For example, you will only be entitled to unemployment benefits if you can show that you are genuinely trying to get a job. Ask Centrelink for advice.

The end of a maintenance order

You will lose your maintenance if you remarry or start living with someone in a de facto relationship. You will also lose it if the payer dies—although the order should provide that it will continue to be paid from the estate, if there are sufficient assets. You can insure a former spouse's life to protect your maintenance.

chapter seven

ENDING A DE FACTO RELATIONSHIP

Until recently, the ending of a de facto relationship was very different from the ending of a marriage. Basically, the law took very little interest in the process and the couple simply separated, each keeping whatever assets were in their name. If this gave rise to inequality and unfairness, well, in most cases as far as the law was concerned, that was simply too bad—if partners in a relationship wanted to protect their interests then they should do the morally correct thing and get married.

By the 1980s it had become clear that this simply wasn't good enough. Women, in particular, were often in the position of having lived with someone for many years, perhaps raising a family and losing their earning capacity by being out of the workforce, yet if the relationship ended they were left virtually penniless with no right to any property unless it was in their name.

Community pressure led to change and now partners in a de facto relationship have some of the same rights as married partners—although there are still some important differences.

As we have seen in Chapter One, to establish legal rights as a result of a de facto relationship you must normally have lived together for at least two years or have a child.

Separation

Generally, the courts have considered that, for separation to occur in a de facto relationship, there must be an intention to separate, in the same way as in a married relationship. For example, you can't say that you have separated just because one of you goes away on a holiday or moves out temporarily after an argument; there needs to be some indication that you intended the relationship to end.

When the relationship ended may be vitally important.

> James L and Joan L had lived together for a total of thirteen years. After ten years they had separated for a period of six months before getting back together. When they finally broke up they couldn't agree on what property they were each entitled to and ended up going to court. The court said the break meant they had had two separate relationships rather than just one. This meant that in deciding on the property division the contribution each of them made in the first relationship couldn't be taken into account because the first relationship had ended before the de facto relationship laws were enacted. It also meant that the application for a property settlement wasn't made in the required time—because four years had passed since the first relationship ended instead of the required two years.

Other cases since then have had different outcomes but it demonstrates that litigation is risky; if you are in a de facto relationship you should protect your interests by means of a clear agreement as to what is a fair financial arrangement if you separate.

Property settlements

The question of whose name any property is in is more important in the case of de facto relationships than in married relationships. However, if you are covered by a de facto relationships act (everywhere except Western Australia, Queensland and Tasmania) your legal rights to property acquired during the relationship are now more clearly defined and equate more closely to the rights of married couples.

In general, if you have lived together for at least two years, or you have a child, if the relationship breaks down either partner has a right to property acquired during the relationship, irrespective of whose name the property is in, and taking into account the financial and non-financial contributions of each partner to the relationship.

Although in theory this mirrors the *Family Law Act*, in practice the courts interpret it more narrowly so that non-financial contribution (usually from the woman) is often not valued as highly as financial contribution (usually from the man) in the way that has been the case historically. This is reinforced by the fact that, in the Family Court, property settlements on divorce take into account the partners' needs for maintenance as well as a fair division of assets, whereas the de facto relationships acts do not specify that this is a matter for consideration.

The courts have shown a disinclination to include contributions made before you actually start living together in consideration of what is fair. Consequently, if you buy a home and renovate it before moving in together, you may not have any right to a share in it even if you subsequently live together for more than two years and no matter how much blood, sweat and tears you put into making it beautiful. Make sure your name is registered as an owner.

You can make a property claim if:

- one of you lives in the relevant state or territory on the day the application is made; or
- you lived together in the relevant state or territory for a specified time, usually at least one-third of the time you were together; or
- at least some of your jointly acquired property is in the relevant state or territory. (In other words, you don't have to take proceedings in different states just because you own property in different states.)

Relationships of less than two years

Although it isn't wise to rely on it, sometimes you may be able to make a property claim even though you weren't together for the full two years.

> Liane R sold her home so that she could move in with Robert G. She spent $25 000 on improvements to their new home and also paid out $5000 to discharge Robert's debts, including paying his share of a joint holiday. The relationship broke down after little more than a year and Liane applied to the court for an order saying she was entitled to the $30 000 she had outlaid during the course of the relationship. She claimed that if the order were not made it would result in serious injustice even though the relationship had not lasted for two years. The court agreed with Liane and made the order, although the judge said that the contributions that Robert had made to her welfare and that of her son should be offset against the amount he was ordered to pay. Even when this was done, however, Liane's contributions so far outweighed Robert's contribution that she was entitled to $30 000.

Spouse maintenance

New South Wales, the Australian Capital Territory and the Northern Territory have the most comprehensive laws relating to maintenance for a de facto spouse but they still confer fewer rights than for married spouses. The laws are similar but the New South Wales laws are the oldest and they are the ones dealt with here. If you live in the Australian Capital Territory or the Northern Territory you will need to check the detail.

Provided you have lived together for at least two years, or you have a child of the relationship, you can claim maintenance if:

- you can't support yourself because you are caring for a child of the relationship or a child who belongs to your de facto spouse (but not a child who has a different father); the child must be under twelve, or under sixteen if he or she is mentally or physically disabled (any child under eighteen in the Northern Territory);
- you can't support yourself because your earning capacity has been reduced as a result of the relationship and the court thinks it is fair (e.g. if you have spent many years at home caring for the family and so have lost your job market skills). Maintenance awarded on this basis stops after three years from the date the order is made or four years from the date you separate, whichever occurs first;
- you and your de facto spouse have lived in the jurisdiction in which you are making the application for a specified period of time—for example, you must have lived in New South Wales for at least one-third of the time you were together.

You must also be able to establish that you made a substantial contribution to the relationship (although it needn't have been a monetary contribution, it can be staying at home caring for the family). As well, you must be able to establish that it would be unfair in the circumstances if the court did not grant a maintenance order.

Your application must be made within two years of your separation. However, if you can show that you would suffer more hardship than the person against whom you are claiming, you may be able to claim after the two years has elapsed. Your de facto spouse must be able to afford to pay maintenance. You can't apply for maintenance if you have married or entered into another de facto relationship.

These laws go quite a long way towards putting de facto spouses in the same position as married spouses, but they still aren't completely equal. The difference is subtle but can be seen from the way the laws are phrased. The *Family Law Act* imposes a positive obligation on a married spouse to maintain the other spouse according to need and to the extent that they are able to do so. The de facto relationships acts, on the other hand, phrase it in negative terms, that a partner in a de facto relationship is not liable to maintain the other partner except as provided for in the legislation. In practice, this means that, in the case of married spouses, property and maintenance settlements are more a matter of course and the tests as to contribution and the like tend to be applied less rigorously.

> Thelma was a process worker who had worked throughout her relationship with Michael except for periods before and after her two pregnancies. She continued to work after she and Michael separated until she developed a condition that affected her hand and shoulder and ultimately forced her to leave that form of employment. She claimed maintenance, alleging that she could not support herself adequately because of her child care responsibilities. Her application was unsuccessful because the court held that it was her medical condition rather than the need to care for the children which meant that she couldn't work. The court also held that her ability to earn a living had not been affected by the circumstances of the relationship but by other factors.

Tasmania doesn't have specific de facto relationships legislation but there is a limited right to maintenance as a result of a law passed in 1837 which 'extended the rights of wives to concubines'! The wording notwithstanding, it means that you may be able to make a claim for maintenance if you have lived together for at least twelve months and your spouse has left you or a child of the relationship for no reason and without adequate support, has been guilty of cruelty or misconduct so that it is unreasonable for you to continue to live together, or has been habitually drunk for at least twelve months before the application is made.

In Queensland, Victoria, Western Australia and South Australia, de facto spouses have no specific right to spouse maintenance.

Maintenance if you are pregnant

Throughout Australia you may claim child-bearing expenses from the father of your child at any time during the pregnancy or up to twelve months after the birth of the child.

It is usually possible to claim maintenance for yourself for two months before the birth of the child and three months after the birth. You can also claim reasonable medical expenses in relation to the pregnancy.

The court may order a lump sum or periodic payments to be used as maintenance and may impose appropriate terms and conditions.

If you can't wait for the case to be heard before getting financial assistance, it is possible to get an urgent order.

Support for children

If you have a child, even if you can't claim maintenance for yourself, you can claim child support from the father via the Child Support Agency (see Chapter Eight, *When parents separate*).

chapter eight

WHEN PARENTS SEPARATE

The most important aspect of any family break-up is what will happen to the children. Spouses may cease being married to each other, but they cannot cease being parents. In all but a few cases, parents love their children and manage to put their own differences and difficulties aside at least in this respect, and work out what is best for the children.

While they are together, both parents are responsible for the support and welfare of their children. This responsibility continues if the parents separate unless and until the court orders otherwise. Amendments to the *Family Law Act* in 1996 emphasised the 'interests' of the children rather than the 'rights' of the parents. Terminology was changed to make it clear that children are not pieces of property, and words such as 'custody' and 'access', with their proprietorial overtones are no longer used. The principles underlying the 1996 amendments are that:

- children have the right to know and to be cared for by both their parents;
- children have a right of contact with both their parents, on a regular basis;

- parents share duties and responsibilities concerning the care and welfare of their children;
- parents should agree about the future parenting of their children.

Although the court will want to know what arrangements are being made for the children at the time the divorce is heard, and has the right to override these if it considers they are not in the best interests of the children, in practice the court will usually accept whatever you decide, even if the arrangements are unconventional or not what the judge considers are necessarily the best way of handling the matter. This can't be emphasised too strongly. The information below outlines what the court will take into account and the likely basis for decisions—but if you agree on different arrangements or take different factors into account, that will be the end of the matter by and large, and the court will not interfere. Nevertheless, you may find it useful to take into account the issues the court will consider.

Parenting plans

Parents are encouraged to draw up a parenting plan themselves, rather than seek court orders. The plan should cover all aspects of the children's care, including where they will live and what the arrangements are for them to see the parent with whom they no longer live. Once the plan is registered with the court it is binding.

Parenting orders

If the parents can't agree, either parent, a child or anyone who is concerned with the child's welfare can apply to the court to make a parenting order, of which there are various kinds:

- a *residence order* deals with where the children should live;
- a *contact order* deals with the contact the children will have with another person, usually the parent with whom they no longer live, but possibly including grandparents or other people with whom the children have had a relationship;
- a *specific issues order* deals with any other aspects of parental care—for example, the child's education, religion, medical treatment or discipline.

Court orders last until the child turns eighteen, marries or becomes self-supporting.

Whom should the children live with?

Normally it is considered better for the children if they continue to live with whoever has been the main carer. The law makes no distinction between parents but if the main carer has been the mother it is likely, in the absence of any strongly negative factors, to be in the best interests of the children for them to stay with her. But it is by no means unusual for children to live with their father either because the parents agree or the court considers that their interests are best served by this arrangement.

Can the children decide whom they want to live with?

Of course you can allow the children to decide with whom they would prefer to live. Bear in mind though that this can put children in the difficult position of having to choose between you. If the court is involved, the amount of weight the court will give to the children's wishes depends on how old and how mature they are. Normally, a teenager will have more say than a younger child. Children will not be asked to express a view in court but through a counsellor.

Moving interstate or overseas

Unless both parents can agree on acceptable arrangements, in which case the court won't be involved, courts are reluctant to agree to the parent with whom the children live moving interstate or overseas so that it is hard for the children to see the other parent. On the whole, courts prefer not to interfere with people's ability to live where they choose, especially if there is a good reason for moving, but, following amendments to the *Family Law Act* in 1995, there have been some recent cases where the contact parent has had a close relationship with the children and the court has held that the children's interests would not be best served by the residence parent moving interstate or overseas with them.

Eric and Frances came to Australia from Britain in 1980, shortly after they married. They were divorced seventeen years later when their four children were aged between sixteen and three. The children lived with Frances, and Eric had access although after a time he saw only the youngest child. Frances sought permission to take the children back to England where she had better work prospects and the emotional support of her family; her mother had bought a house for them in England and would not ask for rent until she was on her feet and could afford to pay. Frances said that the children would benefit from the move and they wanted to go. Neither parent could afford the fares involved in access visits and, even though Frances offered to forgo child support so that the money could be used to fund travel costs, it was unlikely that the children would see their father more than once a year at the most. The judge refused Frances's application. He said that he was particularly concerned with the likely adverse effect on the youngest two boys of not growing up in close contact with their father—'the importance of a father in the lives of young children is not to be underestimated...

I think the father still has a great deal to offer to all these children, but especially to the two younger ones'.

A different outcome occurred in another case:

Beverley and Barry's marriage was rocky from the start. They stayed together for eight years and had two children but they had little in common and separated many times. When their daughters were five and three, they parted for good and obtained a divorce. The girls stayed with Beverley but Barry had regular weekend access. Six years down the track, Beverley wished to remarry and move from Queensland to Victoria. Beverley's fiancé, whose two teenage sons lived with him, could not leave Victoria because of business commitments. Barry opposed the application saying that it would reduce his access and have an adverse effect on the children. The court found in favour of Beverley on the ground that the interests of the children were paramount. In this case, the court said, Beverley would be devastated if she could not marry her fiancé, and could be expected to suffer a long period of grief making it difficult for her to cope. The court took the view that it was unjustified to claim that Beverley wanted to pursue her own life at the expense of the children, particularly as the marriage had ended more than six years ago and Barry was also intending to remarry in Queensland.

When contact is denied

Parents with a contact order sometimes complain that the residence parent refuses to let them see their child, in defiance of the court. It can be a difficult problem to solve. Fining or jailing the parent is almost never an acceptable solution and these are the main sanctions available to the court. Some parents maintain that they should not have to pay child support if they are never allowed to see the child but it is generally considered that these are separate issues—child support is money for the child and is not intended as a reward or punishment for the parent with whom the child lives. In extreme cases the court can change the residence order but only if it is in the child's best interests. In many instances the only solution is to wait until the child is old enough to make a decision.

Contact and violence

The courts are reluctant to deny a child's right to have an ongoing relationship with both parents but contact may be refused if a parent is abusive or violent towards a child. If appropriate, the court can order that contact takes place under supervision, either by a suitable relative or other person or at a government-funded contact centre.

Changing the children's name

A mother who wants to change the children's name must have the father's consent. If the father refuses consent she can apply to the court, but the court will not agree unless there is a very good reason—a better reason than, for example, the mere convenience of the children having the same name as the mother if she has remarried. If the father has disappeared and is no longer part of the children's life, then a change may be more acceptable.

Adoption by a step-parent

A child can usually be adopted by a step-parent only if the real parent agrees, the real parent dies, or the real parent has disappeared for a long period and cannot be traced. Even in these cases, the adoption authorities generally consider that a child's interests are best served by retaining their links with the real parent and will encourage the step-parent to seek a residence order or other order that acknowledges their role as step-parent but falls short of outright adoption. If you are considering having your new spouse adopt your child, remember that an adoptive parent is regarded in the same way as a natural parent and if this marriage breaks down your current spouse will have a much greater claim in relation to your child.

Rachel's first husband died suddenly leaving her with four children. The youngest child, Belinda, was three when Rachel married Philip. The marriage was happy in the beginning and when Philip said he wanted to adopt Belinda, Rachel was delighted as he was the only father the little girl had known.

Her first husband had left Rachel quite well off and one thing she had always insisted on was managing her own affairs. She was an astute businesswoman and her assets grew substantially enabling her to be the main contributor to a nice home for the family and to send all the children to private schools, which she and their father had agreed they would like to do.

About seven years into the marriage Philip made some bad investments and lost a great deal of money. What had previously been a bad temper turned into violence against Rachel. Shocked at his treatment of her, and after trying unsuccessfully to persuade him to seek counselling, Rachel decided the marriage would have to end. Apart from her own feelings she was not prepared to put her children at risk of violence. Philip sought a property settlement and, to Rachel's dismay, custody of Belinda. Rachel wasn't so wealthy that she could afford to sacrifice too many of her assets and still pay the children's school fees. In any event she considered that, as the money had come from the children's father, and had been managed by her without any input from Philip, he had no moral right to it. Rachel suspected that the custody application had more to do with negotiating a large financial settlement than with real affection for Belinda, but as the child's adoptive father there was no question that Philip had the right to make it. In the end, possibly because by the time the case came to court Belinda was nearly fourteen and able to make her own decision, Philip dropped his custody application, but not before Rachel and the children had been subjected to years of stress and uncertainty and, of course, expensive legal fees.

Abduction of children

About sixty children a year, or more than one a week, are abducted by the non-residence parent. If you think this may happen, get legal advice quickly. You can get a court order and then have the child's name put on the stop list at all exit points from Australia. Your permission is necessary for the child to get a passport. If the child already has a passport the court can order that it be handed over or it can be put on the stop list at the passport office.

If the worst happens and your child is abducted, provided the country to which the child is taken is a signatory to the Hague Convention, that country will order that the child be returned to you. If the country is not a signatory to the Hague Convention, the only way to get the child back is to go there and try to get an order from that country's courts. In either case, you will need legal advice. You may be able to get financial assistance from the federal government to help get your child back—ask your lawyer.

Conciliation counselling

If you can't agree yourselves what the arrangements are for the children you may decide, or the court may order you, to try conciliation counselling. This is a means of solving the dispute with the help of trained relationship counsellors employed by the Family Court. Counselling is confidential and normally lawyers are not present. Counselling is successful in helping parents reach agreement in about seventy-five per cent of cases. If it is unsuccessful, the court will have to decide for you. Court-ordered counselling is free. If you decide to try counselling, ask at the enquiry counter.

Child support

The Child Support Scheme means that the non-residence parent pays a regular amount of money to the residence parent to help with the child's support and upbringing. The scheme can be used by parents whether they are married or unmarried. The scheme means that you don't have to go to court to apply for child support, it is dealt with administratively by the Child Support Agency (CSA).

The Child Support Scheme applies to anyone who separated on or after 1 October 1989 or who has a child born on or after 1 October, 1989. If you separated before this date or all your children were born before this date, you may still need to apply through the court for child maintenance. However, you can have the money collected by the CSA. Note that, if even one of your children was born after 1 October, 1989, *all* your children are covered by the Child Support Scheme.

Children cannot apply to the CSA on their own behalf. However, a child who is not being adequately maintained can take legal action against a parent in the Family Court, although this is rare.

How the Child Support Scheme operates

Under the Child Support Scheme an amount of money, determined by a formula, is paid by the parent with whom the child does not live to the parent with whom the child lives. The formula varies according to different circumstances. The amount of money a parent must pay when the formula has been applied is called an assessment.

To get an assessment, either parent can apply to the CSA. Application forms are available from any branch of the CSA or Centrelink. Once the form has been lodged, the CSA will contact the other parent and arrange for an assessment to be made.

If the parents agree, the money can be paid directly to the residence parent. Otherwise it will be deducted from the non-residence parent's wage and paid to the parent via the CSA.

How an assessment is calculated

The formula that is used to calculate an assessment varies according to the circumstances of each parent. Basically, it takes the non-residence parent's taxable income and deducts an amount for living expenses plus an allowance for each relevant dependent child. If the residence parent's income is above average weekly earnings, another deduction is made, depending on how many dependent children there are. After making all the deductions, a percentage of the remaining income is paid as child support, depending on the number of children. The percentage varies from 18 per cent for one child to 36 per cent for five or more children.

Note that the allowances for children apply only to relevant dependent children. This includes natural or adopted children and stepchildren whom the step-parent is obliged to support as the result of a court order. The allowances do not apply to stepchildren for whom there is no court order or the children of a new partner, even if they live in the same house, unless they are adopted. The theory behind this is that children are entitled to support from their own parents. Children of a previous relationship should be supported by *their* non-residence parent.

In most cases, a child support assessment is reasonably straightforward. However, there are many permutations—for example, to take account of the greater-than-usual time the child spends with the non-residence parent, parents whose income is extremely low, parents whose income is extremely high, lump sum payments and many other circumstances. The CSA can give advice or you can get advice from a lawyer as part of your divorce.

When to apply

You can apply for child support at any time after separation—there is no time limit. However, an assessment can only be backdated for twenty-eight days so if you don't apply early you can't recover what you've missed out on, except for the immediately preceding month.

Objecting to a CSA decision

If you feel that a decision made by the Child Support Agency is wrong, you can object to the Departure from Assessment Team. Grounds on which you can object include the details used in an assessment and decisions that are made on the basis of an application for change as a result of special circumstances.

Some of the circumstances in which an assessment might be altered include a child with special needs (e.g. a handicapped child) or where the costs of access are unusually high (e.g. the non-residence parent lives a long way away).

Child support agreements

Parents are encouraged to reach their own agreement for child support. An agreement must be in writing and once it has been accepted by the CSA it is binding. It is generally best if the agreement is based on an assessment but one of the advantages of an agreement is that mutually agreed allowances can be made for individual circumstances. Acceptance means only that the CSA is satisfied that the agreement complies with the legal requirements; the CSA will not make a judgment about the arrangements.

If you receive social security, an agreement must provide for the amount you are entitled to under an assessment. In other words, you can't agree to little or no child support and then rely on the taxpayer to make up the difference.

If an agreement provides for a lump sum payment in lieu of periodic child support payment, you *must* get legal advice. It is an area in which there are many traps and unless the agreement is very carefully drawn you may find you make a substantial lump sum payment and are later liable for child support as well. If you make a lump sum payment and your child later comes to live with you, you can't get the lump sum back, whereas you can have an assessment varied. On the other hand, if you are the parent with whom the child lives, a lump sum might be better than nothing if you think your ex-partner won't keep up the payments.

> Regina and Peter agreed that Peter would pay $300 a week child support for their two children. Not long afterwards, Peter was retrenched and received a $350 000 redundancy and superannuation payout. At this stage, they went to court. Peter said he should be excused from further child support obligations because his income had dropped so dramatically. Regina said this would be unfair since he now had significant assets, and she sought a lump sum payment. The court agreed with Regina that, in the light of his substantial assets, Peter should still support his children. However, the court refused to make a lump sum order, saying that since Peter could invest the money he had received he should continue to pay the $300 a week. In reaching its decision, the court said there were two circumstances in which lump sum child support would be awarded. The first was where a particular need for the sum arose in relation to the children. The second was when there was a real prospect that the paying parent would not meet the weekly payments.

When child support isn't paid

If a parent defaults on their child support obligations, the CSA will pursue the matter. It is sometimes difficult to enforce payments in the case of self-employed parents since automatic deductions may not be possible. It is also not uncommon for self-employed parents to understate their income to avoid their child support responsibilities. The fact that the CSA is part of the Tax Office with access to tax records makes this more difficult than it would otherwise be but it happens and can be hard to combat.

How long does child support last?

Child support lasts until the child reaches the age of eighteen (or the end of the school year if the child turns eighteen during the school year), is adopted by someone else, or marries. If a child over eighteen has special needs (e.g. for education or is handicapped) it is possible to apply to the court for maintenance under the *Family Law Act*.

part four

Fundamentals

chapter nine

MONEY

Love might conquer all but that usually means all except disputes over money. To say that money is the downfall of many relationships is almost a cliché. But relationships do founder on money matters and, no matter how often horror stories surface or how many warnings are given, couples still clash over money arrangements more than any other aspect of their life together.

If you discuss how you and your partner relate to money and set down some ground rules early in the relationship, you will make better decisions and head off an almost inevitable source of future conflict. Think about your respective 'money personalities'. Is one of you cautious and the other a risk-taker? Would one of you not dream of spending more than you have available at the time, while the other regards being in debt as a natural part of life? Does money burn a hole in your pocket whereas the other can walk around with a wallet full of notes for months?

If you are both working you will need to decide who will pay for what and what proportion of the household expenses each should be responsible for, having regard to differences in your income levels. Women especially need to consider what arrangements will apply if they decide to leave the workforce, either short term or longer term, to have children. If you have led an independent life with your own income, it will be a huge change to be dependent on your partner for support. Even if you continue to work part-time, you will probably have less income than you have been used to. How will you cope with this? Historically, women who want their own money have often been seen as materialistic, but it simply gives choices that being dependent denies.

You will need to think about how the finances are arranged—for example, whether all the money should be placed into a joint account to which you each have unrestricted access, or whether some money should be allocated to each partner for individual, non-accountable spending.

You may need to take your family and cultural backgrounds into account. For example, if you grew up in a family in which thrift was highly valued, you may find it difficult to cope with a partner with a laissez-faire approach to the family finances. In some cultures, money is regarded as something to be shared with the extended family, including parents and siblings. If your partner has grown up in one of these ethnic groups and you come from a more individualistic background in which the immediate family is valued almost to the exclusion of the extended family, think about how you will cope if some seemingly ne'er-do-well distant relative expects your partner to come to the financial rescue.

You should also discuss what goals you each have. Do you want to travel or is it more important to send the kids to a private school? Does one or both of you have a vision of taking some time out in the future to explore some personal passion or simply to get out of the rat race? Of course, you may not be able to answer all these questions early in your relationship, but you can at least discuss what you would do if particular circumstances arise. The very fact that you have considered the issues will make them easier to resolve when the time comes.

How you organise your financial affairs ought to be as much a shared responsibility as any other aspect of your relationship. All too often women, in particular, find out about their partner's financial situation when it is too late, either because the relationship has broken down, their partner has died, or the money has gone and bankruptcy is looming.

Joint bank accounts

Many couples find it convenient to operate a joint bank account on which either can sign, since the normal business practice of requiring both signatures can be a bit cumbersome for routine household operations. If you plan on doing this, be aware that either of you can draw all the money out. So if one spouse decamps to Brazil, they can take all the money in the joint account with them. It is estimated that one-third of spouses involved in relationship breakdowns draws all the money out of a joint account without telling the other spouse. You may think your spouse is one of the remaining two-thirds—well, good luck. And consider the fact that very few lawyers of this writer's acquaintance are prepared to operate joint-spouse accounts!

Obtaining credit

You are entitled to obtain credit on your own account without your spouse's permission or authority. A credit provider who asks for your spouse's signature, if your spouse is not a party to the loan, may be in breach of the antidiscrimination laws.

Credit cards

Ideally, you will each have your own credit card. Regardless of who actually pays the bills, and even if you don't earn much money, having your own credit card enables you to build up a credit record. If you don't have a card and later divorce or are widowed, it may be difficult to get one if you do not earn an income and do not have a credit record.

If one of you has a primary card and the other has a supplementary card, ask if the statement can be issued in both names—this can be useful in establishing a credit record for the supplementary cardholder as well as the main cardholder.

Remember that the primary cardholder remains responsible for paying the accounts. If your supplementary cardholder spouse charges a cruise on the QE2 to your credit card, you can't argue that it was without your authority—you will have to pay the bill. Be aware also that cancelling a supplementary card, even in writing, may not be sufficient to stop it being used—you may have actually to get the card back and return it to the card company.

> When James L and his wife separated he cancelled his wife's supplementary American Express card and thought that was the end of the matter. However, his wife arranged to have another card sent to her without his knowledge. Six months later she ran up $1500 worth of expenses on the card, and the bill was sent to James. He refused to pay. However, he was told that according to the terms of the contract he was liable and furthermore that any future purchases would be his responsibility too. It wasn't possible to cancel the card and the only way he could escape liability was to return the card to American Express. James sought legal advice and eventually the situation was resolved in his favour—but it was a difficult and expensive exercise.

Sexually transmitted debt

This phrase has been coined to describe the all-too-common situation where one spouse becomes responsible for the debts of the other spouse. At the very least you should practise safe credit and avoid being caught.

There are two vitally important points to bear in mind:

- you are not responsible for your spouse's debts simply because you are a spouse;
- you are only responsible for your spouse's debts if you sign something that says you accept responsibility (i.e. you have to take a positive step).

The most common ways one spouse becomes responsible for the other spouse's debts are:

- signing a credit agreement as co-borrower;
- agreeing to guarantee a loan.

Co-borrower

If you are both earning and have agreed to share expenses, signing a credit agreement as a co-borrower may seem like good sense. It simply means that you are each responsible for half the debt, right? Wrong. In law, it means that you are each responsible for *all* the debt. 'Jointly and severally liable' is the legal term and it means that, if you default on the loan, the finance company has the right to recover the entire amount loaned plus interest from either borrower. So if you borrow $30 000 to buy a car and your spouse disappears with the car, you may have to pay off the entire amount of the loan still outstanding—even though you no longer have the car.

Going guarantor

Going guarantor can be an even greater source of angst. There is a common misapprehension that the guarantor is giving a kind of testimonial for the character of the person borrowing the money. That is wrong, wrong, wrong! You are guaranteeing the *money* not the borrower. If the borrower can't pay, you are undertaking that you will pay. Only go guarantor if you trust your spouse implicitly, you can afford it, and you are sure you will be able to afford it for the duration of the loan (you are not planning to have a baby, for example).

And don't sign while you are stirring the soup or feeding the baby—take the time to make sure you understand exactly what you are committing yourself to. There are numerous cases where a woman has found that her home was mortgaged as security for a business loan without her really understanding that it was at risk, or that she had borrowed money without fully realising the implications. The first she knows about it is when the bank forecloses on the mortgage or assets are repossessed.

If you give a personal guarantee it probably means that all your personal assets are at risk. Unlike a mortgage over a house, where only the house is at risk if there is a default under the loan, with a personal guarantee everything owned by the guarantor can be at risk, including property, cars, shares, jewellery, furniture. It is not uncommon for the owners of a small business to be asked personally to guarantee the debts of the business to the bank or other finance provider. Guarantees are often unlimited and may cover future debts as well as debts existing at the time the guarantee is given. For example, if you guarantee the lease payments on a business car, your guarantee may cover all cars leased in the future from that credit provider. If you and your spouse own a business together, make sure you know exactly what the financial arrangements are.

The fact that you resign your directorship of the company (e.g. if you and your spouse separate) doesn't necessarily mean that you are released from any guarantee you have signed. In a recent case the court held that a man who had resigned as director of a company was still bound by a guarantee he had given for the company's overdraft, not only in relation to the overdraft that existed at the time but also in relation to increases in the overdraft that occurred after his resignation. Before signing any guarantee, talk to your lawyer to make sure the conditions you are agreeing to are reasonable.

A recent case that gives some hope to women who do sign a guarantee has proved somewhat contentious, with feminists divided on whether women should any longer be able to claim special protection.

When Jocelyn separated from her husband, she remained living in their home in one of Sydney's affluent suburbs, taking over the mortgage. Two years after the marriage ended she thought she had put the past behind her—until, out of the blue, she was notified by the bank that they were calling on a guarantee she had signed during her marriage to enable her husband to finance a business venture to the extent of $370 000. There was no way Jocelyn could find funds of this kind without losing her home and she asked the court to release her from the guarantee.

Jocelyn was a professional who had several substantial investments and was a director of a company. Despite her considerable business acumen, the first court said that in signing the guarantee she had been guided by matters of the heart rather than the head; she was influenced by the fact that her husband consistently told her that she was a fool in business matters, and she was trying to save her marriage; she did not fully understand what she was signing and should therefore not be liable to pay the money due under the guarantee. The bank appealed and won. Jocelyn took the matter to the High Court and eight years later was released from her obligation.

The court re-established a sixty-year-old principle that banks have no right to recover money from married women who guarantee their husband's debts, if they did not know what they were letting themselves in for. J's husband had told her that the guarantee carried no risk 'because if the money isn't there, the gold is there'. The bank neither explained the transaction to J nor did it make it clear that the guarantee was secured by the family home. Under the circumstances, the court ruled that she should not be liable for the money owing.

Most cases, however, come down on the side of the bank and the woman is tipped out of her home.

Now divorced, Dorothy was married over thirty years ago and was a traditional homemaker, rearing her children instead of pursuing a career. She had been living in her home, worth about $220 000, with a $58 000 mortgage, for twenty-one years. During her marriage, Dorothy had signed the guarantee documents for her husband's business and when it failed the bank demanded nearly $782 000 from her. Dorothy was appalled and claimed that the bank and the accountant had failed to explain to her the impact of the guarantees she was signing. She said that the guarantee was harsh and unconscionable. In this case, the judge found for the bank. The judge said that Dorothy must have known that her debt to the bank was for the full amount of the loan and not merely for the $58 000 mortgage on the house. He said that there is no obligation for a bank to ensure that a guarantor obtains independent legal advice, or to explain the effect of the guarantee.

Dorothy is exploring avenues of appeal but has no money to pay for solicitors' and barristers' fees. So far a local solicitor friend has conducted her case. The bank employed senior counsel, two junior counsel and two solicitors. Dorothy says that her ex-husband did not deliberately exploit her; it was simply bad luck that his business failed. That, however, is of no relevance to the bank—it proposes to get its money in whatever way it can.

A little more protection exists if you go guarantor for non-business purchases, such as a car, that are covered by the Consumer Credit Code. The Code provides that:

- the guarantee must be written and signed by the guarantor;
- the guarantee must be easily legible and clearly expressed;
- the amount required under the guarantee may not be more than the borrower is liable for;
- if an extension of the guarantee is sought, the credit provider must give the guarantor a copy of the contract and obtain the guarantor's written acceptance;
- if an increase in liability is sought the credit provider must give the guarantor notice in writing and the guarantor must agree in writing;
- enforcement expenses may only be those reasonably incurred.

Under the Code, if enforcing the guarantee will cause you to suffer personal hardship (e.g. because you are ill or have lost your job) you may have the right to have the contract varied to take account of this so that payments are reduced or suspended until you get back on your feet.

Just sign here, darling...

In many family businesses, one spouse, usually the husband, runs the business and the other spouse is simply a 'silent' partner, having no involvement in or knowledge of the business. The husband makes all the business decisions and, when necessary, presents his wife with relevant documents and a request to just sign here, darling...'.

Never sign any document that you don't understand even if your spouse says it is only a formality with no serious implications. If you feel shy about questioning your spouse, ask yourself how your spouse would react if the position were reversed and you were asking him for a signature. Would he simply sign without question? It is not disloyal to want to protect yourself from financial ruin.

Until recently, having both spouses as the nominal owners of the business was often the only practical way to comply with the law which required that all companies needed at least two directors. Now the law has been changed so that small, private companies need only one director. If you are a director of a family company but play no part in the business and don't want to, have it changed.

An added reason for not being a non-involved director is that the courts are taking a much tougher line with all directors. As far as the law is concerned, if you are a director of a company you are expected to be familiar with the operations of the company and it is no excuse to say that you have had no interest in it and have never been actively involved in it.

> In a landmark case in Victoria, the Supreme Court held that a widow, Mrs M, was personally liable for $165 000 owed by a company of which she was a director. The circumstances were not unusual. A family company, KM Trading Pty Ltd, had been established by Mrs M's husband to run a group of tobacco kiosks in Melbourne. When Mr M died, the couple's son had taken over the running of the business, and Mrs M had had even less to do with it than when her husband was alive. She occasionally signed a document when it was put in front of her, but that was all; her son no longer insisted that she receive regular reports as to the state of the business, as his father had done. Mrs M was getting older, and she was more than happy to leave everything to her son. The business did not prosper under the son's management and eventually, when stock was bought from a major tobacco supplier, the company was technically insolvent, so that it was unlikely to be able to pay the bill. Even though Mrs M had no idea the company was in financial difficulties,

the supplier successfully sued her, and she had to sell her personal assets to meet the claim.

A family business

Often spouses go into business together in a real sense and both are deeply involved in business operations. There may be a spouse partnership, for example, in running a franchise or other retail outlet, or one spouse may manage the business, often in cases where the other spouse is a professional such as a doctor, or a tradesperson such as a builder or a plumber.

These arrangements usually work well and are both financially successful and personally rewarding. It is important, however, to make sure that the business is properly structured and operates in the same way as if you were not related. In the most successful businesses each person's roles are clearly defined.

In a management arrangement, it is important that the tasks be defined and appropriately rewarded. Women sometimes do the books, answer the phone and undertake other essential administrative tasks for nominal remuneration. All contributors to the business should be paid according to market value if the business can afford it. If the business can't afford it—for example, because it is not yet making a profit or has fallen on hard times, then all contributors should make equivalent sacrifices in remuneration.

If you are going into partnership, you should have a partnership agreement setting out whether it is an equal partnership, who owns how many shares, how the accounts will be kept, who can sign on the company account, whether two signatures are necessary for cheques, how disputes will be resolved and, importantly, what will happen if the partnership is dissolved—and given that 80 per cent of all new businesses fail and nearly 40 per cent of all first marriages also fail, it is the ultimate in ostrich-like behaviour to think it can't happen to you.

If you don't have a written partnership agreement, the law of partnerships lays down some basic rules. Some of the important ones are:

- *All partners are entitled to share equally in any profits* made by the business and must *contribute equally to any losses*. This is one of the matters that are often changed by a partnership agreement. If one of you puts in more capital than the other, it might be agreed that the greater contributor should get a greater share of the profits.
- *Each partner is wholly responsible for all the firm's contracts and dealings.* This means that you are bound by an agreement signed by your spouse and vice versa, including in relation to money you borrow. One of the important features of a partnership agreement is usually to limit the extent to which one partner can suffer from the possible bad judgment or behaviour of another partner, but it is virtually impossible to avoid liability completely and, if you don't trust your spouse's business judgment, don't go into business together.
- *Each partner is equally responsible for the firm's management*, and is entitled to participate in it.
- *Each partner has a right to see the firm's accounts*, which must be kept at the place of business.

General business arrangements

Even if you aren't in business together, if you make any business arrangements with your spouse take the same precautions as you would in any other circumstances.

> Anna was a successful chiropractor in an affluent suburb. Starting from scratch, Anna had worked hard to build up her business

and when she and her husband of five years, Ron, decided to have a baby, the practice supported three chiropractors and other providers of health services. Anna arranged to take a year off when the baby was born, confident that her business was in good hands. A week after she brought the baby home from hospital, Ron told Anna that his computer consultancy was going through a temporary bad patch and he needed an injection of funds to help him get back on his feet. Anna readily agreed and arranged for the money to be transferred to his account.

Six months later, Ron had lost not only his money but hers as well. Anna could no longer pay her staff and was forced to close her practice. Unable to accept that his own business failure had caused the downturn in their fortunes, Ron became abusive to Anna and after several months of his treatment she decided that she could no longer continue with the marriage. She was now in a position where all her hard work had come to nothing, she had no practice generating an income, she had a twelve-month-old baby to support and a limited capacity to work because of the demands of motherhood. Initially, she took a job with someone else and then, when her son was about three, she managed to open her own practice again. After two years, the practice is proving successful but it is very hard work and it will be some time before she is financially secure once more. She says she will never be so trusting again.

Remedies for unfair contracts

Be under no illusion that it is better not to sign a contract in the first place than to rely on being able to get out of it. In particular, you can't get out of a contract after you have signed it just because you later decide you don't like what it says. Nevertheless, if the contract is very unfair it is sometimes possible to have it overturned by the court. The legal term describing unfair conditions is 'harsh and unconscionable', and it means very oppressive and unjust, not just difficult or inconvenient to comply with.

Giovanni and Cesira Amadio were a typical Italian migrant couple. Now in their seventies and with little formal education, they had worked long and hard in their market-garden business to make a good life for them and their four sons. They were especially proud of their second son Vincenzo, whose ritzy parties and glamorous lifestyle clearly indicated his prosperity and success with his building company. When Vincenzo came to them and said he had struck a sticky financial patch and needed them to guarantee a temporary loan by the bank to tide him over, they agreed to help out. They were told the loan was for a maximum of $50 000 for six months.

Vincenzo arranged for the bank manager to visit his parents with him, and they signed the guarantee, secured by a mortgage over some property which provided their retirement income. The senior Amadios spoke little English, and completed the formalities as the bank manager and their son instructed them. A few months later, the Amadios' world collapsed. Not only was their son in default on the loan, they found that the amount at stake was not $50 000 as they had been led to believe, but $240 000. Furthermore, at the time of taking out the loan their son was not merely experiencing temporary cash-flow shortage—his business was virtually insolvent, a fact of which both he and the bank were aware. The bank had been helping him daily to maintain the appearance of prosperity by dishonouring some cheques drawn on his account and meeting others so that critical creditors were paid.

The bank gave notice that it intended to enforce the guarantee. The Amadios decided to fight. Five years later, in a landmark decision by the High Court, they won. The Court said the Amadios' lack of English was a special disability. It must have been obvious to the bank that they were unaware of what they were getting into, and under the circumstances the bank had a clear obligation of disclosure. It would be, in the Court's view, unfair and unconscionable for the bank to be allowed to enforce the guarantee. The Amadios were released from their legal obligations under the contract.

Superannuation

There are two aspects to superannuation: making provision for your own superannuation on retirement, and your rights in relation to your partner's superannuation.

Women, typically, are disadvantaged by superannuation funds which are predicated on long-term continuous membership. For the most part, women have at least some time out of the workforce while they have children and may have some years of part-time work. Few funds meet these needs although it is improving. Before joining a super scheme, check with an independent adviser that it suits your requirements.

If you are married you are normally entitled to a proportion of your husband's super if he dies. The amount depends on the scheme.

If you are a de facto spouse you may not have the same built-in rights to your partner's superannuation as a married spouse. Fund managers normally have wide powers to exercise their discretion in favour of a dependent de facto spouse and, if you have been in a long-standing relationship at the time of your partner's death, you may have little trouble establishing a claim. But you will have to establish the claim, produce evidence as to the length of your relationship and so on, unlike a married spouse who can claim as of right. The only way to make really sure of access to your partner's super is to be named as a beneficiary in the policy.

Recent amendments to the law mean that it may be possible for you to make contributions to your partner's super fund, irrespective of whether you are married and regardless of whether your partner is working, provided they are under the age of sixty-five. This means not only that you can top up your partner's contributions but you may also be able to continue to make contributions if your partner becomes unemployed.

Power of attorney

A power of attorney is a legal document that allows someone else the right to manage your affairs and sign documents on your behalf. It should only be given with very great care to someone you trust implicitly. Normally, you will only want to give a power of attorney if you are going overseas or you are ill. In these circumstances, the power of attorney can be limited to what you want to achieve (see also Chapter Twelve, *Growing older*).

Bankruptcy

If you and your spouse are partners in a family business that goes to the wall, you can both be made bankrupt (even if you don't know much about the business). In essence, going bankrupt means that you haven't any hope of paying your creditors and your assets are taken over by a government official who has the power to sell them to pay your debts. You can be made bankrupt by your creditors or voluntarily on your own application.

Many restrictions apply to a bankrupt. In particular, you must surrender your passport, you must get permission from the court to travel out of Australia, and you may not obtain credit for more than $3000 without telling the creditor that you are bankrupt. As well, you may not manage a company, you must advise the person who is managing your affairs if you move house, and you must provide information about your income and dependants as required.

If your spouse goes bankrupt, your assets can't be seized to pay their debts. However, anything your spouse has given you within two years of the bankruptcy can be taken back and sold. In some circumstances, gifts given to you within five years may be revoked.

There are certain assets that can't be sold. These include normal household furniture and effects and a motor vehicle up to the value of $5000. However, the family home may be sold, if it is in your spouse's name. If you own the home jointly with your spouse, their share will be sold unless you can buy it out. If the sale goes ahead, you will be paid your share of the proceeds.

If you fail to keep up the mortgage payments on your home, the mortgagee is a secured creditor and can take possession of the home, unlike other creditors who must be satisfied with whatever payment eventuates from the sale of assets.

Your spouse may also have to put part of their after-tax income towards meeting their debts, depending on how much they earn and how many dependants there are, so you may find that the family income is substantially reduced.

Your ability to obtain credit should not be affected by your spouse's bankruptcy. If you are refused credit and think that it may be because your spouse is bankrupt, contact the antidiscrimination office—the person who refused you credit may be guilty of indirect discrimination at the very least.

Under normal circumstances, bankruptcy ends after three years. Going bankrupt is normally a last resort but it has the advantage that it may enable you to make a fresh start. Part of the reason for the bankruptcy laws is to provide an orderly means by which creditors can be dealt with as fairly as possible, while at the same time enabling the debtor to escape from a hopeless financial situation.

Jennifer and Robert lived together for seven years and had three children. Jennifer had bought clothes and household goods on several store accounts that she operated. Then Robert left. Jennifer was forced to rely on social security to survive and had no hope of paying off the money she owed. The stores where she had bought the goods threatened legal action. Jennifer went to a credit advisory service and was advised to go bankrupt. She didn't own the home, she had no other assets of any significance and there was little likelihood that she could get a job in the foreseeable future. By going bankrupt, she forced the stores to withdraw their legal action. She felt bad about taking this course of action but she really had little choice. She was never going to be able to repay the money, even if the stores had been able to proceed with the legal action and were granted a judgment against her. By going bankrupt it removed the pressure and she could get on with her life.

A cautionary tale

With any financial arrangement at all, even if it seems to be for your benefit, make sure you get the best advice possible.

When Fernanda's marriage broke down, she earned her living working as a cleaner. She worked hard and lived frugally, and in a couple of years she had saved enough to put a deposit on a modest home. However, when she applied for a loan the bank would not accept that her financial situation was sufficiently stable and said that it would only grant the loan if she bought the home jointly with her son. Her son agreed to this and Fernanda lived happily in her home for over ten years, making all the mortgage payments herself, without any help from her son. She also paid for many improvements and the home was her pride and joy.

Then her son's marriage broke down. It was a bitter divorce, and his wife refused to let him see their young daughter. In retaliation he refused to meet his child support payments. Eventually, the Child Support Agency took legal action against him for non-payment and sought to sell up his assets. His main asset, according to the legal documents, although he had contributed not one cent to it, was the home he owned jointly with his mother. It was a complicated situation and Fernanda considered taking the matter to court. However, she had little money to pay the costs of a court battle and in the end Fernanda sold her home.

chapter ten

SEX

We don't normally think of something as fundamentally human as sex as having a legal aspect—but it has. Mostly the laws relate to young people who, according to our community standards, need special protection from sexual exploitation. Other laws don't relate to sex *per se* but to violence in a sexual context.

At what age can you have sex?

The age at which young people are free to have sex is called the age of consent. Different states have different ideas about when young people are mature enough to be sexually active. If a young person below the specified age has sex, that person is not committing an offence but the person who has sex with them might be.

In most states the age of consent for sex is sixteen, except in South Australia and Tasmania, where it is seventeen. There is sometimes some leeway in the case of young people over the age of about fourteen, especially if there is a difference in age of only a year or two between the people involved. The law is usually brought into play when an older person has sex with an underage person and in this case, the penalties will be more severe the younger the age of the underage person. A child under twelve is considered incapable of consenting to sex; in other words, even if they say they consent, the law takes the view that they are too young to know what they are consenting to and so the consent is invalid. A person who has sex with a child under the age of twelve is likely to be dealt with very severely indeed.

Different age limits apply to homosexual activity. In New South Wales girls can consent to a homosexual relationship at the age of sixteen although boys must be eighteen. Most other states provide that both girls and boys must be eighteen before they can consent to sex with a member of the same gender; although, in line with the tradition established by Queen Victoria, sometimes homosexual relationships and girls aren't dealt with at all—the only age of consent relates to boys.

Contraception and abortion: consent

If you are going to have sex it is essential to use a contraceptive to avoid pregnancy. You can become pregnant from one act of intercourse. You can buy condoms and spermicidal creams from a chemist or supermarket without a doctor's prescription or having to prove your age.

If you want to go on the pill you will need to visit a doctor or family planning clinic. Sometimes parents will help with this and, if they do, there is no problem. The question of how old you must be to get contraceptive advice without your parents knowing is linked with the general issue of consent to medical treatment.

The general age of consent for all aspects of life is eighteen. Once you reach this age, your parents' consent is no longer necessary for whatever you wish to do. However, medical treatment is usually considered to be in a special category and you may be able to give your own consent to medical treatment, which includes contraceptive advice, below the age of eighteen.

The age varies according to the state you live in: for example, in New South Wales the age of consent to medical treatment is fourteen while in South Australia it is sixteen. Other states don't specify a particular age but it is accepted that a person can consent to medical treatment provided the doctor is satisfied that they are mature enough to understand what they are doing and the nature of the treatment. Usually, a young person of fourteen is considered to be mature enough but some doctors feel this is too young; in this case you probably need to be sixteen before the doctor will give the necessary prescription or treatment.

Family planning clinics will normally give contraceptive advice regardless of your age, on the basis that the need to avoid an unwanted pregnancy is the more important consideration.

The doctor should treat a request for contraceptives in confidence, even if the doctor doesn't want to give you a prescription. If you don't want your parents to know, tell the doctor.

You are entitled to your own Medicare card once you turn fifteen. If you are over fourteen, the doctor can bulk-bill Medicare for your treatment without advising your parents.

Just as with contraception, the age of consent for abortion is normally about fourteen, provided the doctor will agree. It is, however, a matter for the doctor and some doctors won't perform an abortion on a young woman under the age of about sixteen without parental consent. In Western Australia girls under sixteen must have the consent of their parents or the court. Some doctors have moral or religious objections to performing an abortion on a woman of any age and in this case, they are entitled to refuse to carry out the procedure. Whether the doctor agrees or not, your request should be treated in confidence and your parents not informed against your wishes. Irrespective of your age, a family planning clinic will refer you to a doctor who performs abortions.

There have been no cases in Australia in which the age of consent for either abortion or contraceptive advice and treatment has been tested. However, because our courts often give considerable weight to decisions in English cases, a case that eventually reached the English House of Lords gives some indication of what might happen here:

> Mrs Gillick had ten children, including five daughters, and she objected to a Department of Health memorandum saying that doctors could give contraceptive advice and treatment to girls under sixteen. She felt so strongly about the matter she took the matter to court, asking for an order forbidding the area health authority from giving such advice to any of her daughters, while they were under sixteen. The case was fought all the way to the House of Lords which dismissed the application saying that parental powers over children dwindle as children grow up and their right to make their own decisions increases. The House of Lords made the following points:
>
> - the doctor must decide that the young person is capable of understanding the moral issues as well as the nature of the advice;
> - the doctor cannot insist that the parents should be informed either by the young person or by the doctor;
> - young people are just as likely to have sex without contraceptives as with them;
> - contraceptive advice or treatment is in a young person's best interests and without it a girl's physical and mental health are likely to suffer.

Abortion: legality

The question of whether abortion is legal is a different issue not related to age of consent. In general, in Australia, an abortion is lawful if the doctor honestly believes it is necessary to preserve the physical or mental health of the mother. In practice, abortion is generally available on demand and, although precise figures are impossible to obtain, estimates have been made of up to 100 000 abortions being performed annually.

There are some indications that a less liberal view towards abortion is emerging. The Australian Capital Territory has recently passed a law providing that a woman seeking an abortion must be given information outlining the medical risks of terminating a pregnancy and shown photographs of the foetus at various stages of its development. The ACT law also insists on a seventy-two hour 'cooling off' period before the abortion can be performed. At the time of writing the law has not been enacted.

Sometimes, greater restrictions apply to performing an abortion when the pregnancy has gone beyond a certain stage. For example, to carry out a late-term abortion the doctor may have to be satisfied that the abortion is necessary to save the mother's life rather than her physical or mental health, and the operation may have to be performed by a qualified gynaecologist or obstetrician. From a medical point of view, the earlier an abortion is carried out the safer it will be. Many doctors will not agree to perform late-term abortions because of the risks involved.

Abortion and fathers

So far, the courts have taken the view that the mother's right to decide whether to have an abortion overrides any view the father may have. A father cannot force a woman to have an abortion, and neither can a father stop an abortion.

> In a case in Queensland, T became pregnant as a result of one act of intercourse with K. T decided to have an abortion, giving as her only reason that 'it would be best for everyone'. K applied to the court for an injunction to restrain T alleging that the abortion would be unlawful. One of the arguments put by K was that an unborn child's life should be protected by the court which is in the role of *parens patriae* (literally, parent of his country). The case went to the High Court which rejected the argument, saying that 'a foetus has no rights of its own until it is born and has a separate existence from its mother'. The court said that this was not to say that a foetus cannot acquire rights on birth with reference to something which happened prior to birth but that while still a foetus, it has no standing in law. Other later cases have had the same result.

Sterilisation

In theory, whether to be sterilised is a matter for a woman or man to decide for themselves. All sterilisation operations should be regarded as permanent, although they can now sometimes be reversed using modern microsurgery techniques.

The simplest way to sterilise a woman is to tie her tubes. In practice, most doctors won't sterilise a young woman under about thirty-five, unless there are medical reasons to do so, for the fairly obvious reason that she may change her mind at a later stage, and modern methods of contraception are extremely reliable. Most sterilisation operations on men consist of a vasectomy in which the tubes carrying semen from the testicles to the penis are cut and tied.

The sterilisation of very young people is normally only considered if the person is intellectually disabled and unable to take responsibility for contraception. Before 1992, it was only necessary for a parent or carer to find a sympathetic doctor to perform the operation. However, in a landmark case in that year, the High Court changed this.

> Marion was thirteen years of age and intellectually disabled. She had begun to menstruate but was incapable of caring for herself physically and of understanding the nature and implications of sexuality, pregnancy and motherhood. Her parents thought she should have a hysterectomy. The Full Court held that the parents could authorise the operation. However, the Department of Health and Community Services appealed to the High Court which decided that a child's interests should be protected by requiring permission from a court. The two main reasons the High Court gave for its decision were that in deciding whether a young person should be sterilised there is a significant risk of making a wrong decision and that, if a wrong decision is made, the consequences on the young person's life would be extremely grave. The judges emphasised that court permission is only required when sterilisation is proposed for non-therapeutic reasons and is not simply the by-product of treatment for some disease or medical condition...

As a result of this decision, if a woman is incapable of giving informed consent to sterilisation either a court or, in some cases, the guardianship board must give permission. The court or board must make a decision based on the best interests of the woman concerned. There may also be a requirement that no other form of contraception is likely to be successful. In New South Wales it is necessary to show that the procedure is necessary to save the woman's life or prevent serious damage to her physical or mental health—and since this is rare, it is rarely worth seeking permission. A carer who disagrees with a decision of a lower court or tribunal can appeal to the Family Court.

In February 1995 the parents of a 17-year-old intellectually-disabled woman were refused permission by the NSW Guardianship Board to have a hysterectomy performed on their daughter on the grounds that the board was not satisfied this was the best form of treatment. The parents then applied to the Family Court which approved the procedure as being in the best interests of the young woman.

Sexually transmitted disease

Sexually transmitted diseases include HIV/AIDS, hepatitis B, syphilis and gonorrhoea. If you acquire a sexually transmitted disease, the doctor must report it to the health authorities. Depending on the state, the doctor may not have to provide your name or other identifying information.

The doctor must also tell you what you can do to avoid infecting anyone else, what the treatment options are and what your responsibilities are. It is your responsibility and not that of your doctor to tell your partner that you are suffering from the disease. If, once the disease has been diagnosed, you infect your partner you may be legally liable and sometimes guilty of an offence.

Sexual assault

Everyone has the right to say yes or no to sex. A person who forces another person to have sex against their will is guilty of sexual assault, which is a serious criminal offence.

If you are a victim of sexual assault you may wish to report it to the police. In this case, you are entitled to ask to be examined by a female police officer. In metropolitan areas specialist sexual assault units, often attached to major hospitals and staffed by women, will provide sympathetic treatment and advice as to the available options. In country areas, where the police station may only be small, obviously you can only be examined by a female officer if one is employed at the station.

Most sexual assault victims want a medical examination to ensure that any physical injuries are detected and treated. You can have a forensic examination carried out at the same time to collect evidence of the assault. This involves the taking of appropriate swabs as well as a blood sample and ideally it will be carried out within seventy-two hours of the assault.

If the offender is caught the police will charge him. However, the case can only proceed if you agree to give evidence. Apart from your own sense of justice, it is important for society that as many perpetrators of sexual assault as possible are dealt with by the law. However, be aware that it may not be easy—despite modifications to the law, some sexual assault victims still complain that they feel they are on trial and not the accused. In particular, although your previous sexual history is not allowed to be brought up in evidence, the question of consent is obviously critical to the defence and you may be cross-examined aggressively on this point.

Incest

Sex between related family members, such as parent and child or brother and sister, is incest and is against the law. Sex between people who are not so closely related—for example, a step-parent and stepchild or uncle and niece—is not, strictly speaking, incest but, at least where young people are involved, is regarded as sexual abuse and will be severely dealt with if it comes before the courts. There are increasing numbers of cases where women who have been sexually abused in their childhood by a family member or close family friend are taking legal action many years later.

Other situations when sex isn't allowed

Apart from underage sex and sex between close relatives there are other circumstances in which sexual relationships are either ethically or legally prohibited. These occur when a power relationship exists so that the weaker party may be exploited by the stronger party. Such relationships include students and teachers, and doctors and patients. In these cases, the offender can be brought before the court and charged with an offence.

chapter eleven

VIOLENCE

Barely five years ago, an Australian survey yielded the astonishing information that one person in five thought it was acceptable for a man to hit his wife. It is difficult to imagine that if those who expressed this view were assaulted as they walked down the street they would not be outraged and anxious to see the offender brought to justice. The fact that violence between spouses is apparently different raises some fundamental questions about the relationship between women and men.

But perhaps we shouldn't be surprised. Tolerance, if not outright acceptance, of male spousal violence has a long history. In 1768, William Blackstone, in his classic *Commentaries on the Laws of England*, wrote of a husband's right to use moderate chastisement in order to enforce obedience by his wife to his lawful commands. 'Moderate chastisement' was defined by the courts as using any reasonable instrument including 'a rod that was no thicker than his thumb'.

In its 1990 report, *Violence: Directions for Australia*, the National Committee on Violence recognised domestic violence as 'one of the most entrenched and pervasive forms of violence in our society'.

Statistics in the area of domestic violence are understandably flimsy, since many cases of spouse abuse are not reported. However, a survey conducted by the Australian Bureau of Statistics in 1996 found that nearly a quarter of women who are married or in a de facto relationship have experienced violence by their partner at some stage of the relationship. Over three-quarters of women who are murdered are killed by their partners.

An assault is no less an assault because it happens between partners. If you are in a violent relationship, get help. Domestic violence laws are aimed specifically at solving some of the problems that arise because of the fact that the relationship is ongoing.

Laws can't solve all problems though. Court orders can be ignored by someone really determined. Don't add to the statistics of women who have been murdered in spite of taking all the legal options available. If you are caught in a situation of extreme violence, or threatened violence, the only sensible course of action may be to get out.

Domestic violence isn't just physical assault, it includes sexual assault and emotional and psychological abuse. It also includes threats of violence. Domestic violence laws depend on the state you live in but the broad principles are the same.

Immediate help

If you are being assaulted, or think you are about to be assaulted, ring the police as quickly as you can. Give your name and address and tell the police it is urgent. For the most part the police take immediate action when they receive a domestic violence call but, if they don't come within a short period of time, ring again and keep ringing until they do come. In many areas there is a domestic violence liaison officer attached to the police station and, if you don't get a satisfactory response, ask to speak to this person. There may also be a domestic violence hotline that operates twenty-four hours a day—the number will be in the front of the phone book. If you are in a situation where violence is possible, keep the phone number of the local police station handy together with the hotline number. If you don't have these numbers you can dial 000.

In almost all circumstances of domestic violence, the police have the right to enter your home so don't be intimidated by a spouse who says he won't let them in. Even if your spouse owns the home, if you are being hurt the police can come in. If necessary, they can get a warrant over the phone. Apart from dealing with your spouse, the police can help you to leave and take you to a safe place, such as a refuge, or to stay with a friend. The action they take may depend on you. The police can't do much if you seem uncertain in your attitude. If you want your spouse charged, make that clear.

If a charge is laid, your spouse will be arrested, taken to the police station, finger-printed, photographed and formally charged. He may then be allowed out on bail, although not if the police consider he is likely to attack you again.

Restraining orders

Domestic violence cases require two different outcomes: to protect the victim and to punish the offender.

To get protection you should ask the local court for a restraining order. These orders are called by different names—for example, in New South Wales they are apprehended violence orders and in Victoria they are intervention orders. But, whatever they are called, the orders try to stop your partner from assaulting you. The violence doesn't actually have to have taken place for an order to be granted; you only have to establish that you are afraid it will take place and that your fear is reasonable.

A restraining order can be tailored to suit your circumstances. For example, it may simply provide that your partner must not assault you, or it may provide that he does not live in or approach your home, or that he does not approach you or your children wherever you are. The orders are not limited to spouses or partners; they can also be sought by parents against children, or children against parents, indeed by anyone who is afraid of being attacked by another person, even if there is no family relationship.

Nor do restraining orders have to relate to violence in the normally accepted sense of assault. You can get an order if your partner is harassing you, for example, by stalking you or making unreasonable or threatening phone calls. Stalking means following you or waiting outside your house or place of work, or behaving in a threatening or otherwise intimidating way.

Once you have a restraining order, if your partner disobeys the order he can be arrested and charged with a criminal offence. This means that the police don't have to wait for you to be assaulted before they can make an arrest; if your partner comes to your home when there is an order forbidding it, your partner can be arrested.

Make sure you have a copy of the restraining order. It is also a good idea to check in with the police. They should have a copy of the order too (the court will normally send one) but if you make yourself known to them they are more likely to be alert to the fact that you may possibly need help, and conscious that your situation is regarded seriously by the court.

Getting a restraining order is often an effective way of stopping a violent spouse. Once the man sees that you are serious, that you are prepared to take action and make known to the authorities and other people what is happening, he may back off. It has been estimated that 90 per cent of restraining orders are successful in this way.

Applying for a restraining order

Sometimes the police will apply for a restraining order on your behalf. However, it is easy to apply yourself. All you have to do is go to the local court and ask the clerk of the court or the chamber magistrate what to do. They will listen to your story and, provided they are satisfied that you genuinely fear for your safety, they may prepare the necessary documents while you are there. If you have already been assaulted or even threatened with assault, it will help to establish that your fears are well founded if you have a note of the dates and some brief details of what happened.

Once you have established your need for a restraining order, the court will issue a summons requiring your partner to appear in court when the matter is set down for hearing, usually in a couple of weeks. Although your partner is given this opportunity to put his side of the case, if he doesn't turn up (and many men don't) the court can then grant the order without further delay.

If the situation is urgent, you can get a temporary order immediately. This means that the court won't wait for your partner to give his side of the story but will grant the order at once. In this case, the order will only be for a short period of time, until a hearing can be arranged. At the hearing, if the court is persuaded that the danger is real, despite hearing the other side of the story, it will extend the order.

A restraining order is effective as soon as your partner receives the documents. It isn't effective before this so you may need to stay with a friend for a day or so until the order has been served. The court will arrange for the documents to be served—you don't have to do it.

Laying charges

The second purpose of the domestic violence laws is to punish the offender and, if the police attend a domestic violence attack, your partner may be charged. Usually the police will ask whether you want charges to be laid. There isn't much point in the police charging your partner if you don't want this to happen, since the success of the case will depend on your giving evidence in court.

Need for evidence

Before the court will convict anyone on any charge, there must be evidence establishing the person's guilt. Of course, the police will provide some evidence if they have attended the assault. However, it helps if you can also supply evidence. Always see a doctor, even if you don't think it is necessary from a medical point of view. If you can, get someone to take photographs of your bruises and other injuries. Increasingly, the police are supplied with a polaroid camera, so they can take photos of you and of the scene. If you have a neighbour or family member who can support your evidence, that may be helpful. Remember, the chances are that your partner will try to persuade the court that he is blameless and if it is only your word against his, with no supporting evidence, it is difficult for the court to convict him.

Requirement to give evidence

In most states, the decision as to whether to give evidence against your partner is yours. If you don't want to, you don't have to. The position is different in New South Wales where you can be required to give evidence.

This apparently odd state of affairs arose because in some cases, when the police attempted to take action after a domestic violence complaint, not infrequently the woman was subjected to further violence or intimidation by the man or his family until she agreed not to give evidence. If she had no choice, the reasoning went, there would be no point in the intimidation. However, a woman who is a genuinely reluctant witness may not give effective evidence anyway, so whether the provision is utilised depends on the situation.

Sexual assault

Sexual coercion is domestic violence too. Your partner or spouse does not have any more right to force you to have sex than a person who is unrelated to you. At one time, because sex was considered to be a husband's 'right', there was no such offence as rape within marriage. There is now. A spouse or partner who has sex without consent can be charged with sexual assault in the same way as a spouse or partner who beats you up. If your spouse is unhappy with your sexual relationship, the remedy is to leave and seek a divorce after twelve months.

Provocation

In recent years the courts have shown a willingness to accept the so-called 'battered woman' syndrome as a defence to murder or serious bodily harm. This is based on the long-standing principle that provocation may be a mitigating factor in cases of violence and, under some circumstances, a defence to murder. Typically, provocation has been used by men who have killed a spouse after discovering her in a sexual relationship with someone else. With the advent of the women's movement, women argued that a similar defence should be available when a woman killed her partner after years of violence, even if the killing did not happen in the heat of the moment. It was pointed out that if a woman tried to retaliate as a violent incident was taking place, she would probably be killed herself because of her lack of comparable physical strength. Even so, after years of intimidation and violence, a woman could 'snap' in the same way as a man and be driven to murder, even though actual violence was not taking place at the time. It is a defence that sometimes has mixed success.

> Heather Osland and her twenty-year-old son, David, were subjected to thirteen years of physical and sexual abuse by Heather's husband, Frank Osland. She was raped, punched, kicked, beaten and had a gun held at her head. She wasn't allowed to go to sleep before Frank did. He pushed her head into the bathwater if she filled it too high. He beat, starved and killed family pets. The children had to witness this cruelty or be beaten themselves. Heather tried to leave but was hunted down. Her attempts to get police help were unsuccessful. Eventually, after digging a grave in the nearby forest, she and her son laced Frank's dinner with a sedative before bashing him to death while he was sleeping. They were tried together and Heather was convicted. However, the jury couldn't agree about David's guilt and at a second trial he was acquitted on the ground of self-defence. Despite an appeal to the High Court, Heather is serving her fourteen-year sentence. At the time of writing, women's groups are agitating on Heather Osland's behalf to have her released.

Violence to children

Children are even more entitled than adults to be protected from domestic violence. The one place a child is entitled to feel safe is at home. No child should have to put up with any form of abuse, physical, mental or sexual, and if a parent thinks a child is being subjected to abuse it is up to them to do something.

If your children are being assaulted, contact either the police or, if the children's physical protection isn't a matter of urgency, it may be more appropriate to contact the welfare authorities. Sometimes, there are special police units to deal with child mistreatment and these will not necessarily take criminal action. They may assist with accommodation, getting medical advice, counselling for the child and anything else that is appropriate.

Women's refuges

Women's refuges are run by women for women and provide short-term shelter for women and their children who are threatened with violence. You can usually make contact with a refuge at any hour of the day or night. Addresses aren't usually published to protect the women in residence but phone numbers are listed in the front of the phone book. The staff are experienced and sensitive and will give support and advice about what to do.

Limits of the law

Despite the legal remedies available for victims of domestic violence, there are limits to what the law can achieve. The fact that an order has been made does not guarantee that it will be complied with. Women and children have been murdered while a man is subject to a court order saying he must stay away from them. Often the only real remedy is to try to establish a new life somewhere else.

part five

Ageing and death

chapter twelve

GROWING OLDER

If parents have obligations to their children, the question can reasonably be asked whether children have obligations to their parents, especially as they get older. In some societies the wisdom and experience that comes with age is venerated, but not, for the most part, in our society. In this country, youth is all and the aged seem often to be treated as if they were expendable.

Unfortunately, benign neglect sometimes becomes active abuse and, although laws are there to protect everyone in the community, it is often virtually impossible for a frail aged person to make use of them. If an old person is physically immobile, it may be difficult to get legal help, accusations are often hard to substantiate and the old person may no longer have the capacity to communicate in a way that enables them to be believed. Of course, if their mind is no longer functioning properly they have virtually no chance of making their predicament known.

Although the moral and ethical answer may be that children do have an obligation to care for a parent who becomes unable to care for him or herself, the law is largely silent on the matter. For the most part, if a child chooses not to take responsibility for a parent, the parent will have to rely on the state.

Whether you are getting older yourself, or have ageing parents, it pays to be aware of the legal ramifications of various decisions that may need to be taken.

Accommodation

Where to live is an important feature of most older people's lives. Retirement will almost certainly be a time when housing needs are reassessed. If you choose to stay in your own home, you may wish to modify the house so that it is easier to live in and maintain.

If you intend to make any structural alterations, you must get permission from the local council. If permission isn't obtained, the council can force you to have the work demolished or redone to conform with council regulations. For do-it-yourself renovations, unless they are very minor, special permission may be needed from the builders' licensing authority—it depends on the amount involved and state regulations.

Letting a room

If you live alone you may wish to let a room in your home, so that you have companionship and help available in the case of disability or illness. Such arrangements often work well but caution is obviously called for. If the prospective tenant or boarder is a stranger, arrange for a trial period before a firm commitment is made. Always have a formal agreement, preferably drawn up by a lawyer, clearly setting out what the arrangements are and (especially) how the agreement can be ended.

Retirement villages

A retirement village is a community of mostly retired people, who live in a complex, usually developed by a private developer or by a church or charitable organisation. There is normally a choice of accommodation options ranging from self-care to nursing home, with hostel or serviced apartment accommodation as an in-between stage. Most villages have self-care and hostel accommodation, but not all have nursing homes attached. The absence of a nursing home within the complex often looms large in the minds of prospective residents, but remember that only seven in every hundred people require nursing home care, and if a village is otherwise suitable it may be worth deferring that problem until it arises.

The location of the village may be a more important consideration. If only because of the amount of land required for development, many villages are on the outskirts of the main centres and, as you get older and perhaps unable to drive, you may become increasingly isolated and unable to participate in normal community activities if you are too far out of town. Similarly, long distances can make it hard for the family to visit regularly. Check the proximity to shops and other services and the availability of public transport, including over weekends.

Be aware that whoever owns and runs the village when you buy in may change. If the developer sells the village to someone else, the new owner may have a different management policy. There may not be a lot you can do about this, except to check before you buy whether there are any plans for sale.

There has been some recent regulation of the retirement village industry which has overcome problems that initially caused dissatisfaction. Legislation may cover charges, maintenance fees, the types of services to be provided and the nature of the title or tenure you are granted. Usually, a statement of your rights must be included with the contract. Depending on the state, the law may provide that you must be allowed a certain time to get adequate legal advice after being given the contract. For example, in Victoria you must be given the contract at least twenty-one days before you sign; in New South Wales you must be given a reasonable time to get legal advice. Similarly, there may be provision for a cooling-off period after you have signed the contract, usually about three to five days (fifteen days in South Australia), during which you can change your mind and cancel the contract without penalty or with only a small penalty.

Nevertheless, despite the outlawing of many practices that were clearly unfair, retirement village contracts should be considered in the same way as any normal property transaction in which it is up to the buyer to ensure that the contract they are signing is acceptable. If you intend buying into a retirement village, get good legal advice from a solicitor who is familiar with this type of transaction.

Legal structures

In most cases, the arrangement by which you acquire the right to live in a retirement village unit will be different from buying an ordinary home unit. In part, this is to enable the developer to exercise more control over the complex and, for example, specify a minimum age of entry, usually about fifty-five. Broadly, the different forms of 'ownership' are strata title, licence, leasehold and company title.

Strata title is the closest to buying an ordinary home unit in that you acquire freehold title to the property and enter into a management agreement for the provision of services and facilities. The advantage is that any capital gain may be yours (although there is often some provision for the developer to retain a proportion of the capital gain, to fund further development). The disadvantage is that it is entirely up to you or your family to sell the unit and this is sometimes difficult, perhaps because of entry restrictions or a reputation for not-so-good management, which may have changed after your purchase. With some other forms of ownership, selling the unit is a matter for the management, at least after a certain period of time.

A *licence agreement* gives you the right to occupy your unit under certain conditions. The agreement you sign will set out your rights.

A *long-term lease* means that you pay market value for a unit in return for a ninety-nine-year lease and the right to use the village facilities. Ownership of the unit remains with the developer (or whoever they sell it to).

Company title means that the developer retains ownership and sells off shares in the company. There will be a separate occupancy agreement giving you the exclusive right to occupy your unit.

Make sure you fully understand the system that applies in your case. They all have advantages and disadvantages.

Entry fees

Normally, a capital sum is paid to buy into the village. These entry charges vary according to how luxurious the units are. At present, one-bedroom units range from about $50 000 to $250 000. Church or charitable organisations have developed villages with lower-priced units, ranging from about $10 000 to $150 000. Entry into these villages may be means-tested.

Weekly fees

Over and above the entry fee, there will be a weekly amount payable for rates, upkeep and maintenance, in much the same way as owners must pay a levy in a normal home unit complex. However, because you are buying a package of accommodation plus care and support facilities, there will be an extra weekly charge to cover these. By and large, the amount will depend on the extent of the services. For a serviced apartment, the weekly fees will probably be higher than for a self-care unit to cover the increased range of services, such as cleaning, provision of meals and so on; however, entry fees are normally lower.

Be aware of how the weekly fees are set and what provision there is for them to be raised. Clearly, as time passes, costs increase and so the weekly fees will be increased to take account of this—but if they rise too steeply it might be hard to find the money from a fixed retirement income. Weekly fee increases are sometimes limited by law, unless agreed by residents, but such a provision will usually give the village the right to withdraw services if they can no longer afford to provide them. Depending on the contract, maintenance fees may be payable until the unit is sold, or for a specified period, whichever occurs first, even if you are no longer living there.

Deferred management fee

As well as the capital cost and general maintenance costs, most privately developed villages charge management fees. These fees may be deferred until the unit is sold. Normally, a deferred management fee is calculated as a percentage of the capital value of the unit combined with the number of years you have lived in the unit. Find out what the percentage is and whether it is calculated on the original purchase price or the resale price. Some schemes work on the basis that the deferred management fee does not increase after a specified number of years.

Repayment of your capital investment

In nearly all retirement village schemes some means of generating funds for future development will be built into the system of finance. Consequently—unlike ordinary property which you simply sell when you no longer want it, receiving the proceeds yourself—when you sell a unit in a retirement village there may be some special arrangement with the owner of the complex. This may mean that you will only get some of the sale price. The costs that may be deducted include:

- the cost of refurbishing the unit;
- the cost of selling the unit;
- a percentage of the capital gain;
- the deferred management fee.

Make sure you understand this and accept it. In particular, take account of the fact that, if you aren't entitled to at least a significant proportion of the capital gain, you may not be able to afford to buy somewhere else if you decide you don't like where you are.

Resident participation

Normally, residents must be given a say in the running of a village. This includes lifestyle matters but it may also involve the right to see the annual budget and accounts. If you have this right it is worth exercising. If there is no provision for resident participation in a village you are considering, think hard about proceeding.

Termination of the contract

Your home in a retirement village isn't quite your castle in the same way as a home to which you have freehold title. In certain circumstances, the contract can be terminated and you can be asked to leave. However, in most cases, the conditions under which this can happen are limited to a serious breach of the contract or residence rules, or a deterioration in your health so that the facility is unsuitable. If there is a disagreement as to whether the contract should be terminated, management may have to seek independent medical advice or refer the matter to a tribunal.

Disputes

If you have a disagreement with management, first check whether your contract or the by-laws have a provision for dealing with disputes. If there is no such provision, the government may have a system of resolving disputes. This may be a specially appointed referee, it may be a residential tenancies body or it may be the department of fair trading or consumer affairs. Check what procedures you can follow before incurring the expense of legal action.

Your pension

The entry fee you pay to buy into a retirement village is taken into account in assessing your pension. The rules are complicated and you should check with Centrelink as to the effect it will have in your case.

Low-income housing

There are various government housing schemes to assist people on low incomes, including the elderly. These include low-rental accommodation, home renovation aid and rent relief. The housing department or the Council on the Ageing can provide details.

Granny flats

Councils often have less stringent building requirements for granny flats which enable elderly people to live with family members while at the same time remaining independent. It is important to have a clear agreement about any such arrangement. In particular, if the younger couple wish to opt out of the arrangement and sell the property, perhaps because of a marriage breakdown, the occupant of a granny flat may have no legal rights.

Driving

As well as the normal requirements for motor vehicle registration and licence renewal, once you reach a certain age, usually eighty, you will have to undergo a medical test each year before your licence will be renewed. Once you turn eighty-five, you will usually be required to have an annual driving test before your licence will be renewed.

Medical treatment

Older people have the same rights as all other members of the community in relation to medical treatment. In particular, information about a diagnosis or treatment does not have to be disclosed without the patient's consent. Of course, doctors often discuss a patient's condition with close family members where it is obvious that they are in the patient's confidence and consent may be implied. However, families have no automatic right to such information and if the patient asks the doctor not to discuss their condition with the family, the doctor is bound by that.

A doctor must get the patient's consent for any treatment. If the treatment is experimental or controversial, the doctor has a special responsibility to ensure that the patient understands what is being proposed.

If a patient lacks the mental capacity to make decisions, then a close family relative may be able to give consent on their behalf. It is something of a grey area, and sometimes the guardianship board may need to be involved, but in most normal circumstances if treatment is in the patient's interests it is highly unlikely that either the doctor or the relative giving consent would be considered to have acted improperly.

Medical records

Doctors don't have to show patients their medical records or hand them over to the patient. However, if a patient is moving to a different area most doctors will give a summary of relevant health matters to a new doctor on the patient's request.

Commonwealth Seniors Health Card

The Commonwealth Seniors Health Card enables self-funded retirees to get similar health concessions to those available to age pensioners. The card is income tested—at present the income limit for a couple is $67 000. Other limits apply to particular circumstances—Centrelink can supply the details

Home care

There is a range of government services to help frail older people stay in their own home. The Home and Community Care (HACC) program provides help with domestic tasks, transport, food, bathing and dressing. It may also be possible to obtain nursing services, assistance with necessary modifications to the home and respite care. For some services, the local doctor may need to give a referral.

If you need several of these services you may be helped by a Community Aged Care Package (CACP) in which one person coordinates all your necessary care so that you do not have to deal with a number of different people. To be eligible for a CACP you must be assessed by an Aged Care Assessment Team. The fees for these services depend on your ability to pay.

As the carer of an older person you may be entitled to a Carer Payment, depending on the level of care you provide and whether you satisfy an income and assets test. If the person requires a level of care equivalent to that in a nursing home, the carer may be eligible for a Domiciliary Nursing Care Benefit.

For details of all these services, ring the Department for the Ageing or the seniors information service in your state.

Investment advice

The need for good investment advice is probably never so important as when you are older. Investing in an enterprise that fails can be devastating once you no longer have a job income to build up new funds. There have been several notable instances over the past decade where even seemingly safe investments have failed and retirees have lost large sums of money. The investment advice industry is better regulated than it used to be but it isn't foolproof. If you are seeking investment advice, and especially if you are handing money over to be managed by someone else, make sure you have checked their credentials thoroughly.

As far as legal protection is concerned, legislators and regulatory authorities often don't find out about suspect practices until something has gone wrong. By the time laws prohibiting some course of action have been passed, many people have been hurt. Similarly, even if laws exist, unscrupulous operators don't always abide by them, and by the time they are discovered you may have already lost your money. If you plan to invest in an enterprise, satisfy yourself that the directors are reputable and that the company has substance.

Be aware that, beyond a certain point, it isn't possible to pass laws preventing bad management. If a company goes into liquidation so that there is no money in the coffers you may have little hope of recouping your investment. If the directors have been negligent they may face a term in prison, but that won't get your money back.

Legal action for negligent financial advice is hard to sustain. Advice based on bad judgment isn't necessarily negligent advice and provided the advisers had reasonable grounds for their recommendations, suing them will be a waste of time and money.

Management of affairs

If you become incapable of managing your affairs, the family will need to step in. If you have previously made a power of attorney, it will make life much easier, as the person named can simply take over. Remember that an ordinary power of attorney ceases to be legally valid if you become mentally incapable. To overcome this you should make an enduring power of attorney which will come into operation if you become mentally incapacitated. This must be specially drawn and you should get legal advice. You may also want to insist that your partner gives you an enduring power of attorney in the case of their mental incapacity. An enduring power of attorney must be certified by a lawyer.

Until recently, powers of attorney could only deal with financial and legal matters. However, personal and lifestyle matters can now usually be dealt with as well. You may be able to appoint more than one attorney and you can then specify what functions each person has the authority to perform. In these circumstances, your power of attorney will only come into effect if you become incapable of making these decisions for yourself.

If you have not made a power of attorney, relatives may need permission from the court or the guardianship board to take over your affairs. The guardianship board will normally appoint an appropriate family member as guardian. The guardian can manage your affairs and make decisions regarding the care and the services you should receive. A guardian has a legal responsibility to make all decisions in your interests.

> Alan and Jean S were in their sixties and had been happily married for over thirty years. When Alan retired they both looked forward to spending more time together and especially to travelling which they loved. Then, out of the blue, Alan had a stroke. Virtually totally incapacitated, mentally and physically, he had to be hospitalised. All their assets were in Alan's name, including the family home. He thought he had taken care of this by leaving everything to Jean in his will. But he wasn't dead and so the will was no help. Jean could do nothing, she couldn't even pay the bills. In particular, she wanted to sell their home so she could move closer to the nursing home where it looked as if Alan would spend the rest of his life. Eventually Alan's affairs were taken over by the Guardianship Board—which meant that every time Jean wanted to do something she had to ask permission. If Jean had had an enduring power of attorney all this would have been avoided.

Nursing homes

Nursing homes exist to care for people who can no longer care for themselves. Not everyone in a nursing home is old but most are. Nursing homes are run either by the government or private enterprise. Some of the privately owned homes are operated for profit. Others are run by churches or other charitable organisations on a not-for-profit basis. Although, like most institutions, standards vary from excellent to not so good, all nursing homes must be registered and are regularly inspected.

A person will only be admitted to a nursing home if they are assessed as being in need of it on the basis of infirmity, illness, incapacity or disability. The assessment is normally made by the person's doctor together with Aged Care Assessment Teams attached to major public hospitals.

The fees payable in a nursing home depend on when the person was admitted. People who are admitted now pay a basic daily care fee, set by the government. If they are part-pensioners or non-pensioners there is also an income-tested weekly fee.

There is a charter of residents' rights and responsibilities which applies to approved nursing homes and which deals with basic human rights. These include the right to appropriate quality care, the right to be treated with dignity and respect, and the right to be accepted as an individual.

Complaints about nursing homes can be made to the health department or, in New South Wales, the Health Care Complaints Commission.

Accommodation bond or charge

The situation in relation to accommodation bonds and charges is complicated and the amounts will vary according to individual circumstances. This is a broad outline—check the detail with Centrelink or the Council on the Ageing.

An accommodation bond is an amount of money you pay when you enter a hostel (i.e. the stage between self-care and a nursing home). The amount of the bond is determined by the hostel management but you must not be left with less than a specified amount in assets, currently $23 000, but it will change each year. If you are married, only half the family assets are taken into account. The bond is refundable except for an annual amount of up to $2600 which may be deducted for a maximum of five years. As an example, if you pay a bond of

$50 000, the hostel can keep $2600 a year for five years, or a maximum of $13 000 ($2600 x 5). You have six months after you move in to pay the bond and you may pay by instalments or a lump sum. If you pay by instalments, you will normally be charged interest.

If you enter a nursing home, there may be an accommodation charge, if your assets are more than a certain amount, currently $23 000 (single) or $46 000 (couple). The maximum accommodation charge is currently $4380 a year or the margin of assets above $23 000 divided by five years, whichever is the lower. The accommodation charge can be levied for a maximum of five years.

The family home

The family home is exempt from the assets test for the purposes of the accommodation bond or accommodation charge if:

- your partner or dependent child is living there;
- a carer has been living there for at least two years and is eligible for an income support payment;
- a close relative has been living there for at least five years and is eligible for an income support payment.

Different rules apply if the family home is rented out to pay the accommodation bond or charge—ask Centrelink.

Age Pension

If you do not have adequate superannuation when you retire you should be eligible for the age pension. Men become entitled to the pension at age sixty-five. Until recently, women were entitled to the pension at age sixty. However, the age for women is being gradually increased so that it will be sixty-five too. Consequently, at present, the age when a woman becomes entitled to the pension depends on when she was born—Centrelink can supply the details.

The pension is means-tested for income and assets, unless you are permanently blind. To be eligible for the pension, you must be an Australian citizen and live in Australia or conform with other residency requirements. There are certain time requirements that apply to residency and citizenship.

If you and your spouse are separated because one lives indefinitely in a nursing home, each can claim the single rate of pension. If one spouse is in a nursing home and the other still lives at home, the home is not counted as an asset.

Funeral funds

Funeral funds allow you to pay for the funeral before you die. The money is invested by the fund so that it retains its value as far as possible. You can leave the directions for the funeral with the trustee of the fund or in your will. Funerals cost from about $2000 depending on whether you wish to be cremated or buried. Cremations are slightly cheaper than burials. Money invested in a funeral fund up to $5000 is exempt from the Centrelink assets test and from tax.

An advance directive (sometimes called a living will) sets out your wishes about future medical treatment—for example, whether or not you want to be kept alive in the case of a terminal illness. Depending on the state, an advance directive may not be legally binding but it provides doctors with guidance as to your wishes. Usually, an advance directive deals with who you want to make treatment decisions for you, the treatments or medical procedures you object to, and whether you want medical help to be given to prolong your life if you are unlikely to recover. You can obtain an advance directive form from the Euthanasia Society in your state—you may be required to pay

Advance directives

What to do if your spouse or parent dies

- Notify family and friends
- Obtain a death certificate
- Register the death
- Arrange the funeral
- Locate the will and notify the executor
- Notify Centrelink
- Notify banks, building societies, credit unions, debtors and creditors
- Notify any pension sources
- Notify Medicare
- Notify insurance and superannuation funds

the joining fee. Alternatively you can ask your lawyer or the relevant government department if your state has legislated for advance directives or powers of attorney to deal with these matters.

Depending on the state, you may also be able to appoint an enduring guardian or patient advocate to see to it that no extreme measures are taken to prolong your life—choose someone who is articulate and able to argue your case forcefully.

Further information

Matters and services relating to older people are administered by both state and federal governments. You can ring the relevant department directly—they will refer you to the correct number if you are unsure which department is responsible for your query. Alternatively, you can contact your state branch of the Council on the Ageing. In some states there is a Seniors

Information Service. Centrelink has information on pensions and benefits. The numbers can be obtained from the Age Page in the front of the phone book.

chapter thirteen

LOVE AND DEATH

About 40 per cent of Australians die every year without having made a will. Not having a will once you marry and, even more importantly, once you have children, is irresponsible. Feeling 'spooked' that somehow the making of a will might hasten your death, is not a good reason for inflicting on your family the difficulties that not having a will involve, not to mention the fact that if you don't have a will no one will know what you want done with your assets. A will is no different from any other property transfer—it just doesn't come into effect immediately.

Your will and marriage

You must make a new will when you marry because any previous will is usually automatically revoked. It is possible to make a will in contemplation of the marriage but this must comply with strict requirements—do not try to do this unless you consult a lawyer. In general, when you marry it is better to make a new will.

It is particularly important to remember to make a new will if you marry your partner after living in a de facto relationship. Even if you made a will providing for your partner when you were living together, the likelihood is that it will be revoked when you marry and you will die intestate.

Your will and divorce

In most circumstances, your will as a whole remains valid on divorce but gifts to your former spouse are revoked. This means that you should make another will if you divorce since you will have to decide what is to happen to your former spouse's share. Similarly, if your spouse has been appointed executor, trustee or guardian that appointment is no longer operative. If you want your former spouse to remain as any of these things, you should make another will reaffirming the appointment. Gifts or appointments relating to your former spouse only remain valid on divorce if the court is satisfied that you did not intend the divorce to revoke the gift or appointment.

Your will and your family

If you think you can do as you like in your will with your own money, silly you! Present-day law insists that you look after family members and the concept of the heavy-handed father punishing recalcitrant children by cutting them out of the will is difficult to sustain in today's world.

If your will does not provide adequately for your spouse and your children they have the right to claim on your estate. This includes ex-nuptial and adopted children. Stepchildren do not have an automatic right to be provided for in your will but if a stepchild lives with you as a dependant you may have some obligations to them.

While the right of children to be included in a will becomes progressively less as they get older and become self-supporting, if there are sufficient assets the court will sometimes take the view that even adult, non-dependent children are entitled to something.

Under some circumstances, grandchildren may have the right to claim on your estate. You may also have to provide for other people in your household if you are supporting them, for example, an elderly parent. As a rule of thumb you have an obligation to take care of anyone who is dependent on you. In other words, if you are responsible for someone while you are alive, that responsibility continues after your death, as far as it reasonably can.

A former spouse may have a claim on your estate, especially if you have been paying maintenance. This is a matter that should be dealt with in the property settlement when you separate and is a good reason for getting proper legal advice at that time.

If you have a de facto spouse it is especially important to make a will. De facto spouses now usually have some right to be provided for in a partner's will but their position may not be as strong as if you were married.

A person who considers that they have been inadequately provided for may challenge the will—in effect, ask the court to rewrite the will so that they receive more. If, for any reason, you don't want to leave something in your will to someone to whom you have a legal obligation, or if what you leave them could be seen as inadequate in the overall context of your estate, you should get legal advice to make sure that you take all the necessary steps so that your wishes will be carried out without a court challenge. Some of the options are to make a clear statement in your will of what you are doing and why, or for the will to provide that anyone who tries to challenge the will forfeits their entitlement.

Your children

If you have young children, you may wish to nominate a guardian in your will to look after them if anything should happen to you. Obviously, you should think about this carefully and ask the person you choose if they agree; many nominated guardians refuse. The fact that you appoint a guardian isn't foolproof as other people in the child's life can challenge the appointment and the court will decide according to the best interests of the child. However, it will provide the court with some guidance. A common cause of challenges in guardianship matters is when a marriage has broken down and the residence parent nominates as guardian someone other than the surviving parent. If you do this, it is sensible to state your reasons clearly. Most guardianship disputes are solved by mediation rather than a court battle.

Whatever assets you leave your children must be administered by a trustee until the children turn eighteen. Choose the trustee carefully; ideally, it will be someone who has good business sense as well as the welfare of your children at heart.

How to make a will

There are three ways of preparing a will: you can have one drawn up by a solicitor, you can have a trustee company draw it up, or you can do it yourself.

Having a will drawn by a lawyer is normally relatively inexpensive if it is reasonably straightforward, perhaps a couple of hundred dollars. If you wish (although there is no obligation), the solicitor will administer the estate, usually deducting the fee from the estate. Normally, the executor will have to employ a solicitor to do at least some of the work, so this is often a practical option. A trustee company will draw a will for nothing, but will insist on being appointed executor of the estate and will then charge a percentage of the value of the assets. This is normally on a sliding scale and may be about four or five per cent on the first $100 000. Trustees are most useful for estates that involve the ongoing administration of a trust fund for the beneficiaries.

If you want to do your will yourself, you can buy a will form from a law stationer or large newsagent. These may be sufficient for simple wills but once you have a family, and so more than one person to leave your assets to, it is better to have your will professionally drawn.

Making sure your will is valid

Once your will comes into operation, you will obviously no longer be available to clear up any misunderstandings. Consequently, over the centuries, the courts have evolved a set of rules to minimise the risk of argument about what you intended. If your will does not conform with these rules it won't be considered to be a proper (valid) will and you will die without a will (intestate).

To be valid—that is, accepted by the court and able to be put into effect—your will must be:

- *in writing*: this can be handwritten, typewritten or printed;
- *signed*: your signature must be at the end of the will;
- *witnessed*: two witnesses must be present when you sign the will and sign it themselves at the same time. All the signatures must be at the end of the will. You and the witnesses should use the same pen—that makes it more likely that you all signed at once if there is a dispute.

As long as it conforms with these requirements, your will can be a simple statement of what you want. All you need to do is name someone to carry out your wishes (your executor) and clearly state to whom your assets and belongings are to go (your beneficiaries).

Witnesses

A witness should not be someone to whom you are leaving something in the will. If a witness is a beneficiary, they may have to forfeit their inheritance. If this is your spouse, it can be disastrous. In recent years, most state laws have been made less strict in this regard to avoid the obvious injustice that arises if a spouse inadvertently witnesses a will. However, not all states have made the changes and, in any event, a beneficiary witnessing a will creates difficulties. To put the matter beyond doubt, have someone else witness your will.

Witnesses do not have to know what is in the will. They are witnessing your signature, not the contents of the will, and they just need to see you sign it.

The attestation clause

It is important to have a statement that you signed in the presence of the witnesses and that they signed in your presence. If the statement isn't there, the will won't be invalid, but when the time comes for probate the court will require the witnesses to sign an affidavit saying when and where the will was executed. If they can't be traced or have died, at the very least it will delay probate and may mean that your will is invalid.

Note that you have to sign your will in the presence of the witnesses. Don't sign it first and then ask a witness to sign at some later stage. Even if they know you very well, you are putting the witness in the position of having to make a false declaration. Lawyers are sometimes confronted with a client, or the spouse of a client, who has signed the will at home and then asks the lawyer to arrange for a witness. Most lawyers refuse.

The residue

It is important to have a clause dealing with 'the residue' of your estate—that is, everything you haven't specifically mentioned. If you don't do this, anything you leave out will be dealt with under the intestacy laws. For example, if you leave the home to your spouse, your jewellery to your daughter and your car to your son but forget about some shares, the shares will be dealt with as if you had died intestate.

Conditions in your will

You can, if you wish, make a bequest conditional on something else. For example, you can leave the home to your children on condition that your spouse has the right to occupy the home during their lifetime. Don't attempt to do this without a lawyer as it can be tricky. The court won't enforce conditions that are against the public interest or which require the beneficiary to do something illegal. Nor will the court normally enforce an unreasonable condition—for example, that a spouse will forfeit their inheritance if they remarry.

Making a will

A summary of steps

- make a list of everything you own (e.g. property, jewellery, car, investments)
- make a list of any money you owe, including a mortgage
- decide to whom you would like to give something
- decide who is to get what
- draw up the will.

Executors

There is no prohibition on an executor being a beneficiary and indeed it is common for a spouse or other close family member to whom you are leaving a major part of your estate to be named as executor. You can have as many executors as you wish, there is no legal maximum. But too many will be cumbersome. You may wish to appoint two executors—if your spouse is the only one and you are both killed in a car accident, there will be no executor. Your executor must be over eighteen. Before naming an executor, you should ask if they agree—the work involved is not insignificant.

If an executor is a beneficiary, the bequest is normally considered to be in lieu of remuneration for the work in administering the will. There will possibly be a need for a

Rights and responsibilities of executors

An executor has the right:

- to be recompensed for expenses in connection with the administration of the estate;
- to a commission or payment of money if granted by the will, beneficiary or court;
- to apply to the court for advice and direction;
- to be released from liability once their duties are complete.

An executor will be personally liable if:

- they are guilty of fraud;
- they are guilty of a breach of trust;
- they fail to carry out the terms of the will.

lawyer to carry out some tasks and they will usually charge for their time.

An executor is in a position of trust and has a legal obligation to fulfil the role with honesty and care. It can have traps so make sure you understand what is expected of you.

Olive agreed to be an executor of her friend Jessica's estate, together with Jessica's only son, Laurence. Jessica had left significant funds for her grandchildren, naming Laurence and Olive as trustees until the children turned eighteen. Laurence decided to put the money into his own business, saying he wanted to make sure that it would grow into something 'the kids could really do something with'. As far as Olive could see, Laurence seemed to know what he was talking about and in any event she thought he would know how to protect his own children. Then the bottom dropped out of the market, Laurence's business failed and took the inheritance with it. Olive felt badly about it but assumed that Laurence was to blame because it had been his decision. She was wrong. Olive had an obligation to ensure the funds were being invested wisely, especially since Laurence was so closely connected with the business. The grandchildren who were set to benefit from Jessica's estate have grounds to sue Olive for negligence and they would have a reasonable chance of winning.

Who can make a will?

Anyone over eighteen can make a will, provided they are of sound mind. You can make a will before you turn eighteen if you are married (although in most circumstances now you must be eighteen before you are permitted to marry so this provision is not very relevant to couples marrying today).

A simple will

This will (date) is made by me (name, address and occupation).

I revoke all previous wills made by me.
I appoint (names) to be my executors.
I give my jewellery to (name).
I give the rest of my estate to (name)

Signed ____________________ (testator)

Signed by the testator in our presence
and attested by us in the presence of him/her

__________________________ (witness)
__________________________ (witness)

Dying without a will

If you die without a valid will you are said to have died intestate and your estate will be divided up according to certain rules. These rules differ between the states, but normally your spouse has first claim on the estate, usually up to a certain amount, followed by your direct descendants, that is children and grandchildren. After that your parents and other next of kin may be entitled to something. The court will appoint an administrator (the equivalent of an executor) to deal with the estate.

While it is not true, as many people think, that the government gets your assets if you die intestate and your estate will probably go to the people you would want to inherit, the government's idea of the way the assets are divided may not be what you want. For example, your spouse may have to sell the home simply because of the way the assets must be divided. Also the unravelling of an intestate estate is normally more complicated and takes longer than if there is a will. It is unfair to impose such difficulties on your relatives.

Changing your will

If you want to change your will, make a new one. It is possible to change or revoke (cancel) an existing will but strict rules must be complied with. For example, each change must be signed and witnessed as if it were a will in its own right. It is usually safer and easier to start again.

There is no limit to the number of wills you can make throughout your life and you should review your will from time to time, say every five years, since new circumstances may have arisen that mean you need to make a new one. It is important to make sure that each successive will clearly states that it revokes all previous wills.

Testamentary promises

If you are promised something in a will in return for carrying out some action in a person's lifetime, and then find that the promise hasn't been fulfilled, you may be able to enforce the promise even though the person is now dead. For example, if you undertake to look after someone while they are alive on the basis that you will be rewarded when they die, and then you find that they haven't honoured the promise in the will, you can probably enforce the promise.

Foreign wills

A will made by a migrant to Australia in their own country, which is valid according to that country's laws, is valid in Australia even if it doesn't conform with Australian laws. However, it is better to make a new will to take account of the new circumstances that probably exist in Australia. Also it can be difficult and expensive to prove that a will is valid in another country.

Probate

Before an estate can be dealt with the will must be recognised as authentic and the executor must officially be acknowledged as having the right to deal with the deceased's property. This is called probate and is carried out either by the registrar of probate (a court official) or by the court itself if there is any dispute.

Probate is normally a straightforward matter of establishing that the testator has died and the will has been properly signed and witnessed. Sometimes probate isn't necessary: for example, if you are the only beneficiary of your spouse's estate. Even in that case, if a transfer of real estate is involved, probate is usually required. Also banks usually require probate before they will release money.

Until probate is granted, the deceased's assets are frozen so you should make arrangements for any dependants to have money to live on immediately after you die.

Small estates

There are usually procedures so that estates below a certain amount (normally about $20 000) can be dealt with quickly and easily. You can ask the Supreme Court in your state for advice (or the local court if you live in the country).

Dealing with the body

The deceased may have stated what is to happen to their body in the will: for example, whether they want to be cremated or buried. Normally their wishes are followed. However, if the family disagrees, it is up to the executor to make the decision.

Right to die

A person's right to die when there is little hope of any further reasonable quality of life is a question that is being increasingly debated in the community. The question has arisen largely because advances in medical technology now enable people to be kept alive in circumstances that would have been impossible even a decade ago.

In theory, because you have a right to refuse medical treatment, you should have some control over whether you live or die. In practice, the right is not always easy to exercise in situations of life and death, although patients' rights have generally been strengthened in this regard either by specific laws or health department guidelines. In many cases, doctors are no longer bound to resuscitate a patient 'no matter what' and patients have the right to decide whether they should be kept on life-support systems when treatment would be futile. Treatment is said to be futile if it would leave the patient with continuing pain or an unacceptable quality of life, or would maintain a vegetative state with no possibility of reversal.

Of course, if you are terminally ill you may not be capable of making a decision about treatment. To cover this eventuality, it is usually possible at an earlier stage of life to make an advance directive (colloquially sometimes called a 'living will') stating that you don't wish extreme measures to be taken to keep you alive if you are suffering from a terminal illness. Alternatively, you can make an enduring power of attorney appointing an agent (usually a close family member) to make treatment decisions if you become incompetent and instructing that person to direct doctors not to take any extraordinary medical procedure to prolong your life.

The current debate hinges mainly on voluntary euthanasia—that is, whether you are entitled to ask for assistance from a doctor to help you die if you are terminally ill and in extreme pain with no quality of life left. On the one side are those who consider that human life is sacred and must be preserved whatever the circumstances. On the other side are those who believe that once quality of life is no longer acceptable and there is no hope of recovery, the person whose life it is should have the right, if they wish, to call on a doctor to help them die. Even many who don't subscribe to the sanctity of human life theory are worried that once people have the right to die, it will be impossible to stop subtle pressure being exerted on old and ill people by relatives who find their continuing existence inconvenient. Other members of the community counter that this is a problem that can and should be solved and it is not a sufficient ground to deny terminally ill people the right to decide their own destiny.

As it stands at present, doctors not infrequently do help terminally ill patients who wish to die, but it is a grey area and the doctors are open to prosecution. Certainly, treatment that is intended to kill the patient is murder and cannot legally be carried out. However, if treatment is administered for some other purpose, for example, to relieve severe pain, and as a result the patient dies, it is possible that this is not a crime.

Organ transplants

Organ transplants are now commonplace. It is a procedure in which 'healthy' organs are transplanted from someone who has died to someone who will die because of a diseased part of the body.

There is usually provision on your driver's licence for you to indicate whether you consent to body organs or tissues being removed in the event of your death. Alternatively, you can say in your will that you would like your organs to be used to save the life of another person. Even if you express this wish in your will your next-of-kin must usually consent to the organs being removed before the hospital will proceed, so discuss it with them first. Usually this person will be your spouse or, if you aren't married, your parents. If there is no next-of-kin available and after reasonable enquiries there appear to be no objections, consent may be dispensed with.

Generally, you can only be a donor if you are over eighteen and therefore capable of giving valid consent. In certain circumstances you can be a donor if you are under eighteen: for example, if it will save the life of one of your siblings.

part six

The legal system

chapter fourteen

THE COURTS

Because Australia has a federal system of government there are two sets of laws—those passed by the federal government which apply throughout the country, and those passed by the various state and territory governments, which apply only in the particular state or territory. At the time of federation, in 1901, the Constitution identified those areas that were the responsibility of the federal government and those areas that were the responsibility of the state governments. For example, customs, defence and currency were matters for the federal government and education, health and transport were matters for the states. By and large, those divisions still apply although in some instances the states have handed over their powers to the federal government.

One of the areas that came within the jurisdiction of the federal government was marriage, and so the *Family Law Act* has always applied throughout Australia. However, people who weren't married but living in a de facto relationship came under state jurisdiction. This led to the anomaly that children of a marriage could be dealt with by the Family Court whereas children of a de facto relationship had to be dealt with by a state court. Not only did this mean that children of de facto relationships were denied the particular expertise that had been built up in the Family Court but that, not infrequently, arrangements for children in the same family had to be decided by different courts. Consequently, the states transferred their powers regarding children to the federal government and now, when a relationship breaks down, the arrangements for all children affected are dealt with by the Family Court. However, where a dispute arising out of a de facto relationship does not involve children, it will usually be heard in a state court. It should be noted that Western Australia did not transfer its powers regarding children to the federal government, which leads to some differences in that state. However, the situation is complex and, as a practical matter, cases involving children are normally heard in the Family Court in that state also. Similarly a recent High Court decision may mean that some cases will go back to the state courts.

Because there are two systems of government, there have to be two court systems, federal and state, to apply the laws.

The court system

State courts operate at three levels. They have different names in different states, but the basic structure is the same.

The authority that a court has to adjudicate on matters is called its jurisdiction. The jurisdiction of a court may depend on how much money is involved, or, in criminal cases, how serious the crime is. If it is a court in which matters can be originated—that is, where cases can have their first hearing—it is said to have original jurisdiction. If the court can hear appeals from other courts, it is said to have appellate jurisdiction.

Lower courts

The courts that deal with the great bulk of matters, including domestic violence and some family law matters, are presided over by a magistrate and, depending on the state, are called magistrates' courts, local courts or courts of petty sessions. All matters in these courts are heard by the magistrate alone, without a jury. Unless you live in an isolated country area, there will probably be a magistrates' court reasonably near to where you live. Children's courts are a special arm of the lower courts and hear charges brought against children or matters that concern children's welfare.

Intermediate courts

Intermediate courts, which have both civil and criminal jurisdiction, are presided over by a judge, and deal with more complex and expensive cases. They also hear appeals from the lower courts. Intermediate courts sometimes have a jury, depending on the type of matter. These courts are mostly called District Courts but in Victoria they are called County Courts.

Supreme courts

The Supreme Court is the highest court in each state, and hears important or complex cases. Sometimes, the jurisdiction of the Supreme Court overlaps with an intermediate court and a case may be heard in either court.

A major function of the Supreme Court is to hear appeals from lower courts. An appeal may be heard by one judge and then, if one of the parties is still unhappy with the decision, by three or even five judges. The majority view prevails.

A matter that starts in the Supreme Court in front of one judge can go on appeal to more than one judge, sometimes two, sometimes three or five. New South Wales has a special Court of Appeal within the Supreme Court. In most cases, the Supreme Court is the last avenue of appeal. Appeals can only go to the High Court if the case is of general legal or constitutional importance.

High Court of Australia

The High Court is the highest court in Australia. There are seven High Court judges and they may all sit on a case, although it is more common for three or five judges to sit. The majority view prevails. The High Court hears matters relating to the Constitution. Except for constitutional matters, all cases that come before the High Court are appeals. You do not automatically have a right of appeal to the High Court, but must be granted special leave by the Court itself. Special leave will be granted if a matter of particular legal significance is involved.

The High Court is based in Canberra, where it hears most cases. Once the High Court has decided a case, that is the end of the matter, there is no further avenue of appeal.

The Federal Court

The Federal Court of Australia deals with federal laws, with an emphasis on industrial laws and bankruptcy. The Federal Court sometimes hears appeals from state supreme courts on federal matters but for the most part it doesn't deal with matters that arise from personal relationships.

The Family Court

The Family Court has the special task of hearing family law matters. If you are getting a divorce it will be heard in the Family Court, along with associated matters such as property disputes and disputes over children. The Family Court runs free information sessions that deal with issues relating to separation, and tell you how the court operates.

The provision of counselling services is integral to Family Court operations. In some circumstances, especially where there is a dispute over children, the court may insist that you consult a counsellor before it will make a decision.

The Court System

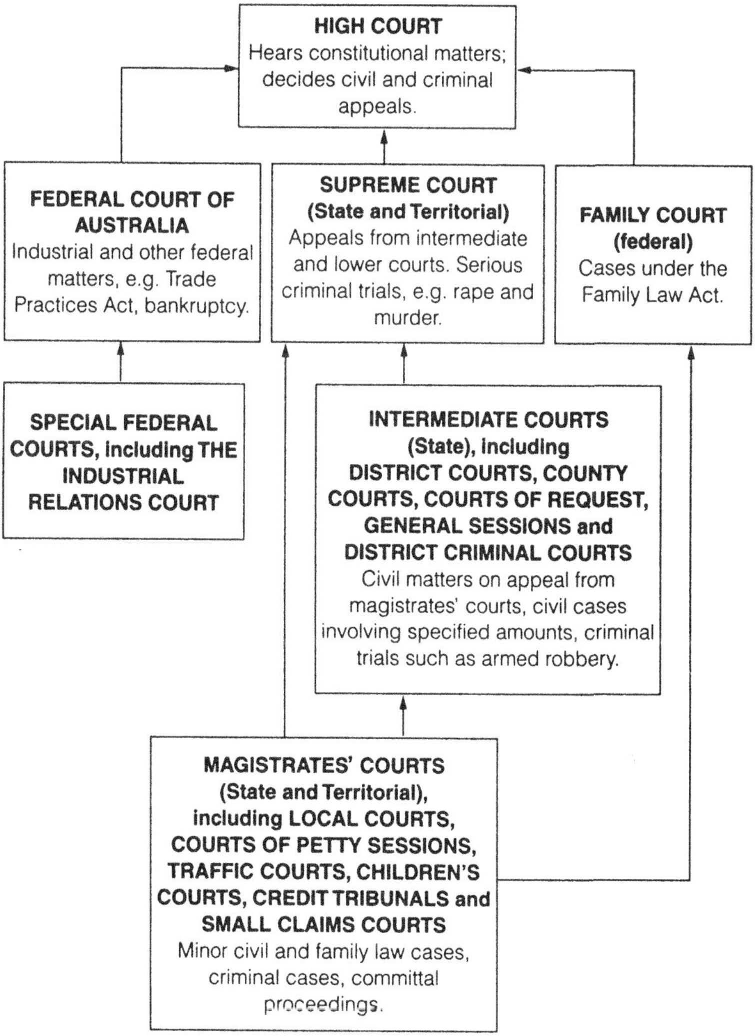

Tribunals

In addition to the main court system, there are various specialist tribunals. Tribunals not only provide expertise on particular subjects, but may also offer a quicker and less expensive way of dealing with a matter. If an antidiscrimination complaint can't be resolved by negotiation it will usually be heard by a tribunal.

Terminology

Court action is called litigation, and the parties are called the litigants. The person who initiates the action is called the plaintiff. The person against whom the action is brought is called the defendant. The plaintiff sues the defendant for compensation or some other remedy for a wrong they believe they have suffered. If the case involves a crime, the action is usually brought by the police and the person charged with the crime may be called the defendant or the offender or the accused—the terms are interchangeable.

When the Family Court was set up it was considered important to avoid the adversarial overtones of ordinary courts, and in that court the two parties to a matter are called the applicant and the respondent. You don't 'sue' someone in the Family Court, you simply make an application for whatever it is you want to achieve: a divorce, an order in relation to a child, a property order or any other appropriate matter. In other courts, the loser is often ordered to pay the winner's costs. Because there are no 'winners' or 'losers' in the Family Court, each side normally meets their own costs.

Access to the courts

In almost all cases, the courts are open to the public. It is fundamental to our concept of democracy that court proceedings should not be held in secret and should be able to be reported, and for the most part there are no restrictions on this.

Because of the particular circumstances that apply to cases that come before them, the Family Court and the Children's Court have slightly different rules. At one time couples seeking a divorce frequently found intimate details of their lives splashed across the front pages of the popular press. Such sensationalism was clearly in no one's interests and, when the *Family Law Act* was passed in 1975, it provided for the Family Court to be closed. However, this meant that the community had little knowledge of the court and came to view its operation with a degree of suspicion. Now the court is open to anyone who wishes to attend. For the most part, however, it is not permitted to identify the participants if proceedings are reported, although a recent change has allowed the publication of names of parents who flout court orders—for example, by refusing contact with the other parent or abducting the child.

In the case of the Children's Court, children are considered to need special protection from possible adverse effects of publicity and, in this court also, it is forbidden to publish any identifying information about a child who is before the court. The Children's Court may be closed if the judge considers it to be in the child's interests.

In all courts, the judge has a discretion to close the court. This discretion is rarely exercised, and usually only with great reluctance. The most frequent cases in which the court is closed are sexual assault cases, especially cases involving incest. Even then, the judge may elect not to close the court but simply prohibit the publication of any identifying information.

Court proceedings

When you file an application with the court asking it to do something, you start 'legal proceedings'. This covers all the formal legal steps you take to get the court to hear your case and make a decision. The terms 'legal action', 'matter' and 'litigation' mean much the same thing.

Before a court can make a decision it needs evidence from the two parties involved about what happened as they see it. Sometimes the evidence has to be supported by other people who are called witnesses.

In most courts, the litigants and the witnesses must usually appear in person so that they can be questioned directly about their evidence. However, in some circumstances, evidence may be presented as a written statement. The statement, which is called an affidavit, must be signed and the person making it must swear on oath that it is true. Of course, a person making an affidavit can be called on to give evidence in person. Affidavits are commonly used in the Family Court.

chapter fifteen

GETTING LEGAL ADVICE

If you need legal advice, of course you will want the best you can afford. Firstly, you need to find an appropriate lawyer and, secondly, you need to be able to pay for the lawyer you choose.

If you don't already have a lawyer, friends or business acquaintances may have recommendations, or you can ring the law society or law institute and ask for two or three names of specialist solicitors in a convenient location.

The legal profession

There are two branches of the legal profession: solicitors and barristers. Their roles overlap to some extent but, when you consult a lawyer, you will see a solicitor. If your case is straightforward, your solicitor will advise you as to the legal position and what action is necessary and may sometimes appear in court on your behalf. This is particularly so in family law matters, where your solicitor will usually handle your case from beginning to end, including court appearances.

If your case is complex the solicitor will probably 'brief' a barrister. The barrister will usually be an expert in the particular area of law and may give a written opinion as to your chances of success in the case. Whatever their area of legal expertise, barristers are court specialists and will normally be engaged if there is a court hearing, except for relatively simple matters in the lower courts and routine divorces in the Family Court. Even in family law matters, if you are fighting over property or the children your solicitor may suggest engaging a barrister. You will need to weigh the cost of a barrister against the value of the case.

Barristers are also called counsel and are divided into senior counsel (SC) and junior counsel. Depending on the state, senior barristers may be called Queen's Counsel (QC). Senior counsel normally charge higher fees than junior counsel. In some states, all lawyers are both solicitors and barristers but mostly they must choose in which branch they wish to practise.

Legal expertise

Make sure your solicitor is expert in the area of law in which you have a problem. For example, if you are buying a house you should look for a solicitor who is expert in conveyancing law; if you are getting a divorce you should look for a solicitor with experience in family law.

The legal profession is less rigidly organised than the medical profession which has a formal system of specialists. Doctors earn the right to call themselves a specialist in a particular field of medicine by undertaking extra years of study with an examination to be passed at the end. Lawyers normally build up areas of expertise simply by practising in that area over a period of time. In some states, lawyers are accredited by the law society once they have practised for a specified period or have undertaken extra courses in their area. Specialist lawyers often advertise in the Yellow Pages or you can ask the law society.

Large metropolitan legal firms are usually divided into specialist practice areas, each with several lawyers who are expert in the relevant area of law. These firms may be more expensive than smaller firms because of higher overheads and also, to some extent, you are probably paying for the name and prestige. These large firms tend to have a strong commercial bias and, for example, many don't accept divorce matters at all.

Legal costs

Legal costs can be expensive but the extremely high fees quoted in the media usually apply to only a few top practitioners and you shouldn't be deterred from getting legal advice if you need it simply because you are afraid of the cost. Depending on the state law society, there may be a rule requiring your solicitor to supply you with a written costs estimate at the beginning of your case. In any event, make sure you ask about fees at your first visit.

Lawyers normally charge by the hour and in fixing their hourly rate they are entitled to take into account the amount of time involved, the degree of skill required and the level of responsibility necessary. Clearly, a junior lawyer will be less expensive than a more experienced lawyer—but remember that the junior lawyer may take longer and so in the end the cost may not be much different. In some matters, including divorce, fees are set down in court scales and these will provide a guide.

If your legal matter involves a dispute with someone else, it may be difficult for the lawyer to provide any more than a rough estimate, since a great deal depends on the behaviour of the other side. For some work, however—for example, making a will or drawing up a contract or partnership agreement—you should be able to get a reasonably accurate costs estimate.

If your case involves an award of money, such as for compensation, in some circumstances your lawyer may agree to act on a 'no win, no pay' basis—but make sure you understand exactly what is involved in your particular case because if you lose you may be required to pay the other side's costs.

It will help to keep lawyers' costs down if you are well prepared in your dealings with them. The lawyer's job is to apply the law to the facts as you present them. Of course, it is part of the lawyer's job to elicit the information they want but it will help if you take any relevant documents with you to the first interview: for example, letters, receipts, a contract, notes that you may have made. Be prepared to answer questions as clearly and concisely as possible.

Except for most divorce matters, if you go to court and win, your opponent will normally be ordered to pay your costs. Be aware that while this will go some way towards covering your costs, it may not cover all of them. The costs you will recover are set down in court scales and if your lawyers charge more than this you will have to meet the extra. Of course, if you go to court and lose, you will have to pay your opponent's costs.

Although a lawyer's bill won't necessarily itemise everything, it should be sufficiently detailed so that it is clear what the charges are for. When you get your bill, if you think you have been overcharged, there are various procedures by which the fees can be checked. Your first step should be to take the matter up with the lawyer but, if you don't get any satisfaction, contact the law society or law institute and ask what you should do. If the fees are unreasonable, you should be able to take action against the lawyer.

Legal aid

Legal aid is a system by which the government pays for a lawyer to represent you in court if you can't afford to pay yourself. Legal aid is means-tested both on income and assets and you may need to show that your case has a reasonable chance of success. Depending on the state, the various legal aid offices differ as to policy and the funds available.

In particular, legal aid is not normally available for divorce. In very limited circumstances it may be available for property disputes and disputes over children but, in many states, funding for these cases is growing harder and harder to obtain and increasingly, legal aid is available only for criminal matters.

You may be able to get preliminary legal advice without charge from a legal aid office on any matter, although again this depends on the resources available. If you think you might be eligible for legal aid or you need legal advice, contact your nearest legal aid office and ask for details.

Community legal centres are another source of legal assistance for low-income earners. These are staffed by both paid and volunteer lawyers and give sympathetic and practical advice including information about how to go about getting legal aid if it is appropriate. Both legal aid offices and community legal centres are listed in the phone book.

INDEX

abduction of a child 110
abortion viii, ix, 27, 45; teenage 62–3, 140–1; legality 142
accommodation, *see* home/accommodation; for the aged, *see* aged
adoption 31, 47–8; in same-sex relationships 38; consent to 55; by step-parent 108–10
age of consent, *see* consent
aged, the Chapter 12; accommodation for 160–7, 171–3, *see also* granny flats, nursing home, retirement village; and family home 173; and funeral fund 174–5; home care for 168–9; information sources for 175–6; investment advice/management of affairs 169–71; medical treatment, *see* medical treatment, consent for/right to refuse
AIDS, *see* HIV/AIDS
antidiscrimination legislation ix, 14, 27, 32, 38, 39–40, 49
anti-vilification legislation 32, 40
Artificial Conception Act, NSW 48
artificial insemination 50, *see also* reproductive technology
assault, *see* violence
Australian Capital Territory, laws in 9, 31, 51, 99–100, 142
Australian Fertility Society 49

baby, having a Chapter 4, *see also* adoption; pregnancy; reproductive technology
bank accounts, joint 121
bankruptcy 134–6, *see also* debt
'battered woman' syndrome 154–5
bigamy/polygamous marriage 19, 21
blood/DNA test for paternity 53, 54
borrowing 123, *see also* credit; debt
business, family/joint 92–3, 124, 127–33
business partnership agreement 129–30

Carer Pension/Payment 36, 169
Centrecare 86
Centrelink 95, 168, 173, 174
child support 75, 94, 100, 108, 111–15
Child Support Act 37
Child Support Agency 75, 94, 102, 111, 112, 113–15
Child Support Scheme 11, 111–15

child/children: abduction of 110; abuse of/violence to 63, 155–6; adopted 47–8, *see also* adoption; and age of consent, *see* consent; birth of, *see* baby, pregnancy; bringing up Chapter 5; contact with parent after divorce/separation 105, 106–8; contraceptives for 63, 139–40; and deceased parent's will/estate 178–9, 180; of de facto relationships 11, 15, 66, 99–100, 195–6; in divorce/separation 77, 79, 82–3, Chapter 8, *see also* maintenance, child support; earnings of 60–1; handicapped 45–6; leaving home 61–2; name/surname of 12, 52–3, 108; nationality of 53; in need of care 64; paternity of 53–5; registration of birth/name 52–3; and reproductive technology, *see* reproductive technology; residence after divorce 105–7, 108; rights of, *see* rights; of same-sex relationships 37; status of ix–x; support of, *see* child support; in trouble with the police 64–5

Children's Court 65, 197, 201

cohabitation agreements 8–11, 32

Community Aged Care Package (CACP) 168

compensation: criminal injuries 13; and same-sex relationships 36; workers, *see* workers compensation

consent, age of: for abortion 140–1; for contraception 63, 139–40, 141; for medical treatment 140–1; for sexual relations 138–9

Consumer Credit Code 127

contact order 105

contraception/contraceptives 27, 61; age of consent for 63, 139–40, 141

contracts, unfair 131–3

Council on the Ageing 172, 175

counselling, marriage 78, 79, 85–6; after divorce 110–11

court system, the 196–200

courts, law: access to 200–1; and divorce, *see* Family Court; proceedings 201–2; and restraining order 150, 151, 152; terminology 200. *See also* Children's Court; Family Court

credit, obtaining 121

credit cards 122, *see also* debt

de facto relationships vii, Chapter 1; children of 11, 15, 66, 99–100, 195–6; death of partner in 4, 14–15, 179; defined 5; discrimination against 13–14; ending Chapter 7; and legal action 195–6; legislation 3–4; maintenance after separation 99–102, *see also* child support; organising finances in 6–11, Chapter 9; property acquisition/ownership in 5–6, 7–8, 9; property settlements 7, 9, 98–9; rights of fathers and grandparents 11–12, 55

De Facto Relationships Act, NSW 4, 31

death Chapter 13; and making a will, *see* will

death of partner/spouse 4, 14–15, 179, Chapter 13; notifications required after 175; in same-sex relationship 33–4; and superannuation 4, 133. *See also* rights to deceased person's estate; will

debt 123–7, *see also* bankruptcy; credit

Declaration of Paternity 54

Disability Support Pension 36

discipline by parents 60

discrimination: against de facto relationships 13–14; against women viii–ix, x, 26–7

divorce 24, 25, Chapter 6; and absent spouse 80–1; application for 79–80; and arrangements for children 77, 79, 82–3, Chapter 8, *see also* child support; and counselling/mediation 79, 85–6, 110–11; and the courts 72–3, 74, 75, 76, 79, 82, 83–5, 86, 104–5; and debts 125–9; 'do-it-yourself' kits 82–3; and family business/company directorship 92–3, 124–5, 128; and the family home 73–4; and finances/property 77–8, 86–95; and furniture 74; law vii–ix; and a lawyer/legal fees 81–2, 205–6;

divorce (cont.)
and living under the same roof 75–6; opposing 78–9, 84; requirements for 78; stamp duty 93; and support/maintenance 75, 93–5; where marriage is less than two years 78; and the will 178, *see also* rights to estate of deceased person's estate
DNA test, *see* blood/DNA test for paternity
domestic relationship agreements, *see* financial agreements in a de facto relationship
Domestic Relationships Act, ACT 31
Domiciliary Nursing Care Benefit 36, 169
driving over the age of eighty-five 167

employment, parents and 56, *see also* women in the workforce
Equal Opportunity Act 27
equality, sexual 25–7
euthanasia 174–5, 190
Euthanasia Society 174–5

Family Court 75, 195–6, 198–9, 200, 201, 202; and child's rights 66–7; and counselling/mediation 79, 85–6; and divorce 72–3, 74, 75, 76, 79, 82, 83–5, 86, 104–5; family home and assets test 173; fees 81; orders re children 104–5; property order in divorce 93; and rights of fathers 11
Family Law Act (1975) 11, 12, 71, 73, 83, 98, 101, 115, 195; amendments 103–4, 106
family planning clinics 140
fathers, rights of 11–12, 55, *see also* parents; and abortion 142–3
fertility treatment, *see* reproductive technology
finances, organising 6–11, 23–4, Chapter 9
financial agreements in a de facto relationship 8–11
funeral funds 174–5

grandparents, rights of 12
granny flats 166–7
guaranteeing a loan 123, 124–7

harassment, sexual 39–40, *see also* discrimination
Health Care Complaints Commission, NSW 172
HIV/AIDS 34, 36, 40, 145
Home and Community Care (HACC) program 168
home care of the aged 168–9
home/accommodation: and the aged, *see* aged; in a de facto relationship 5–8; at divorce 73–4
homosexual marriage 19, *see also* same-sex relationships
homosexuality and the law 30–2, 139
housework 25–6
hysterectomy 27, 144, 145

incest 146
inheritance rights 66, 90–1
in-vitro fertilisation (IVF) 38, 49, *see also* reproductive technology

joint tenancy 6

lawyers, *see* legal profession
legal action 201–2; in de facto relationships 195–6; in marriage 28–9, *see also* divorce; rights of children to take 66–7
legal advice Chapter 15
legal aid 206–7
legal costs 205–6
legal profession, the 203–6
legal system, the Chapter 14
lesbian relationships, *see* same-sex relationships
loans 136–7: guaranteeing 123, 124–7; and unfair contracts 131–3

maintenance/support: in divorce 75, 93–5; at de facto relationship separation 99–102
marriage Chapter 2; age 17–18; to close relative 18–19; and death of spouse, *see* death; and discrimination 26–7; and financial arrangements 23–4, Chapter 9; homosexual 19; and housework 25–6; legal action in 28–9; and making a will 27–8,

177–8; medical treatment in 27; name in 22; notice of intention 19–20; overseas/foreign 21–2; and passport 28; persons authorised to perform ceremony 20; pre-nuptial agreements 23–4; and property ownership 22–3; recognised forms of ceremony 20–1; rights in 25, 26; second 29; sexual relationship in 24–5; valid 19; and wedding ring 21
Marriage Act 30
medical care of children 62–3
medical records, access to 46–7
medical treatment: age of consent for 140–1; for the aged 167–8; consent for 44–5, 167–8; in marriage 27; right to refuse 189–90. *See also* organ transplants
Medicare card 140
Medicare levy 38
mental incapacity 34–5
money Chapter 9, *see also* finances
mortgage payments 6–8, 9, 71

National Committee on Violence 148–9
National Health and Medical Research Council (NHMRC) 48, 49
New South Wales, laws in 3, 4, 9, 31, 38, 48, 50, 62, 99–100, 139, 140, 144, 150, 153, 162, 197
Northern Territory, laws in 11, 99–100
nursing home 171–2, 173; complaints about 172; fees 172

organ transplants 190–1

parental leave 56
parenting Chapter 5
parenting orders: in same-sex relationships 37; after separation/divorce 104–5
parents: and child abuse/neglect 63–4; and child in trouble with the police 64–5; and children leaving home 61–2; and children's earnings 60–1; and children's schooling 59–60; and contracts/leases of under-18s 61; in de facto relationships 12; and discipline 60; and disputes about children 65–6; and employment 56; and medical care of child/children 62; and religion 60; and responsibility for children after separation Chapter 8; rights of 12, 58–9; and teenage abortion 62–3
parents, co- 37
partnership agreement, business 129–30, *see also* business, family/joint
passport 28
paternity of a child 53–5
pension/age pension 173–4; and buying a unit 166
police and domestic violence 149–50, 151, 152, 153
power of attorney 134
pregnancy 9, 43–7; abnormalities 45–6; access to medical records 46–7; birthing options 43; consent for procedures 44–5; formalities at birth 52–5; and reproductive technology 48–9; standard of care 44
pre-nuptial agreement 23–4
probate 188
property ownership: in de facto relationships 5–6, 7–8, 9; in marriage 22–3, *see also* pre-nuptial agreement; in same-sex relationships 35
property settlements: on end of de facto relationship 7, 9, 98–9; on end of marriage 74, 88–95

Queensland, laws in 3, 31, 49, 102

refuges, women's 156
registration of child's birth/name 52–3
Registry of Births, Deaths and Marriages 52
Relationships Australia 86
religion 60
rented accommodation in a de facto relationship 8
reproductive technology 38, 48–52; parentage and consent 50; records and information 50; and surrogacy 51–2
residence order 105, 108
restraining order 150–2

retirement village 161–6; fees 163–4; legal structures/title 162–3; selling a unit in a 164–5; termination of contract 165
rights: of children 57–8, 66–7, 103–4, 108, 178–9; to deceased person's estate 4, 14–15, 178–9, *see also* will; of fathers 11–12, 55, 142–3; of grandparents 12; inheritance 66, 90–1; in marriage 25, 26; of parents 12, 58–9; of terminally ill person to die 189–90

same-sex relationships Chapter 3; and adoption 38; cohabitation agreement 32; and compensation 36; death of a partner in 33–4; discrimination against/vilification of 39–40; fertility treatment 38; and illness 33; and immigration 39; inequalities 31; and insurance and superannuation 35–6; making a will 33–4; and mental incapacity 34–5; and parenting orders 37; and property 35; and social security 36; and taxation 38
schooling 59–60
Seniors Health Card, Commonwealth 168
separation agreements 9–10
sexual assault 145–6, 154, *see also* violence
sexual relations: legal age for 138–9; in marriage 24–5
sexually transmitted disease 145, *see also* HIV/AIDS
Sickness Allowance 36
social security 4, 36, 95
solicitors, *see* legal profession
South Australia, laws in 3, 11, 48, 49, 102, 138, 140, 162
stepchildren and step-parent's will 178
sterilisation 143–5; and the courts 144–5
superannuation/insurance 133–4; in de facto relationships 4, 9, 13; and divorce 89–90; in same-sex relationships 35–6
support, *see* maintenance/support
surrogacy 51–2

Tasmania, laws in 101–2, 138
taxation 38
tenancy-in-common 6

United National Convention on the Rights of the Child 57–8

vasectomy 27
Victoria, laws in 3, 10–11, 38, 48, 49, 50, 102, 150, 162
violence to children 63, 155–6
Violence: Directions for Australia, 1990 report 148–9
violence, domestic 75, 80, Chapter 11; after divorce/separation 108; help/restraining order 149–52; laying charges 152–4; and provocation 154–5

wedding ring 21
Western Australia, laws in 3, 9, 11, 48, 49, 51, 102, 140, 196
will 180–6; changing a 187; and children 178–9, 180; and death of partner/spouse 4, 33–4; and divorce 178; dying without making a 186–7; executors of 184–6; and the family 178–80, *see also* rights to deceased person's estate; foreign 188; and marriage 27–8, 177–8; of a migrant 188; and probate 188; and testamentary promise 187; and wishes of the deceased re the body 189, 190–1; witnesses to 182–3
Wills Act, Victoria 31
women: in the workforce viii, ix, 26, 56; and domestic violence, *see* violence
women's refuges 156
workers compensation in de facto relationships 4, 12

Printed in Dunstable, United Kingdom

91222344R00127